Some Souls Live Forever

Vanessa King

chipmunkapublishing
the mental health publisher

Vanessa King

Published by
Chipmunkapublishing
PO Box 6872
Brentwood
Essex CM13 1ZT
United Kingdom

http://www.chipmunkapublishing.com

Chipmunkapublishing gratefully acknowledge the support of Arts Council England.

ARTS COUNCIL ENGLAND

Some Souls Live Forever

Chapter 1

As the sun cast its rays across the tranquil blue sea, leaving a scattering of sparkles that moved to and fro with the waves, Jessica's thoughts drifted to considering how lucky she was. As she shut her eyes and took a deep breath of fresh sea air, she could feel the sun's beams on her face, warming her cheeks and leaving her with a glowing feeling inside, that felt like true happiness. Beneath her feet, the grains of sand nestled between her toes made her feel calm. It was the feeling of home, and being back made her feel as though her soul was being lifted.

Jessica was a lucky girl. She lived in a beautiful white beach house, positioned not far from a glorious sandy beach that stretched for miles into the distance. Its main living room displayed a huge glassed window that had a view which showed the edge of the sea as its horizon. It was very picturesque. Many days she had spent lying on the soft cream sofa in front of the window, gazing out at the sea wishing she was on a boat sailing out far into the distant horizon. She had lived there since she was born, with her parents, Anna and John, and her older brother Darren.

Every day, before school, Jessica would get up bright and early, just as the sun rose, and she would walk peacefully along the beach. Taking in the ambience, listening to the waves jostle against the shore line and having the deep sea breeze filling her lungs gave her an energy that she could not live long without.

Jessica had been away all summer, on holiday travelling around Italy with her parents. Her dad was an amateur artist trying hard to make it big in the artistic world and to make a mark in history. Accompanied by his family, he had been travelling to several exhibitions in Italy, set in the enchanting suburbs of Venice, and in the contrasting extravagant buildings in Rome. Jessica enjoyed visiting cities; soaking up the culture and enjoying the excitement of visiting different places, but she always loved that feeling of coming home again.

She remembered her friend Blake would be coming round to visit her later that morning. It was two days before school was due to start again. Blake and she had decided, before she went away, that they would make the most of the last two days of the holiday when she returned. Jessica had emailed him from an internet café in Rome telling him when to visit.

As she remembered that internet café now, the enigmatic smells of coffee that had filled that café returned to her. Images filled her mind of the rich, dark, Italian brews being sipped by olive skinned Italians gathered hunched over computers, also writing away, maybe to their friends, or loved ones. One man in particular came vividly to her mind. He had been dressed in a large green trench coat, and with a long black beard. It was so long, that it was tied in a plait at the end, the tip of the plait almost touching the keyboard as he typed. He had such a distinctive look that she remembered it had left her watching for several moments. She remembered him as he typed; obviously unfamiliar with the keyboard, as stretching out from his dark green mittens (which had open ends) were yellow looking fingers, probably from years of smoking tobacco, and with dirty nails. Jessica remembered watching his single yellow index finger punching away at the keys, one at a time, as he struggled to find the keys. He was rather dirty looking, with several earrings punched into both ears, and many torn holes in the black jumper that remained partially hidden beneath his coat. Jessica had wondered what he did for a living. He looked rather like he was a tramp, who Jessica imagined walking up and down the Italian lanes, and sleeping in dirty corners of shops aligning the streets.

Opposite him sat a complete contrast – a clean looking, executive business lady who had brought her own laptop. She had sat dressed in a pink suit, with glasses perched on the end of her nose, her auburn hair fastened tightly with a butterfly grip. Jessica remembered thinking the lady was obviously typing something important, as she leant far forward towards the computer screen with an intent look of interest on her face, typing so fast with her long pink talons and with such a noise, that Jessica felt she was in the midst of a war zone, being gunned down by a machine gun! She remembered wanting to stomp with frustration over to the lady, and pull the plug out of her laptop, because the sound of her talons tapping away on the keys meant that she couldn't concentrate on her own message!

As her thoughts drifted back to the present moment, Jessica remembered she had told Blake to meet her at 10.30am on 30th August, and that was today. As she realised this, she looked promptly at her small red watch hung loosely around her tanned wrist. It read 9.35am. Blake was due to visit at 10.30am. She quickly calculated in her mind that if she were to turn around now and begin walking back home, she could be there for his arrival. Knowing that she was going to soon see Blake again, Jessica felt a warm fuzzy feeling in her chest, a feeling of excitement imagining herself wrapping her arms around his broad shoulders and giving him a big best friend hug, like they always did when they met.

Blake and Jessica had been friends for a long time. He lived at the pale blue beach hut which stood on the bay adjacent to theirs, less than a miles walk from her home. They had met on the beach when they were small toddlers. At the time, his rather less broad shoulders and miniature four year old frame had waddled over to hers and asked her to play all those years ago. It was there they had met, on the sand, with the sea's waves as their accompaniment and the seagulls as their audience, building huge sand castles with long moats that ran out to the sea. She remembered how they always used to love building huge turrets on the castles, and even searching about on the shore for old scraps of wood to use as trap doors. She also remembered their frustration at never quite understanding why the water disappeared from the moat into the sand, no matter how much water they would transport from the sea and pour into the moat with their small yellow buckets. In the end they would always give up, knowing they couldn't make their moat flow with water, and would end up both having as much fun destroying their creations by jumping up and down on them as they did making them!

It had become a family tradition. Realising how well the children used to get on playing with each other, both families used to commune most weekends, letting their children explore and wander. Games of cricket on the beach, Frisbee, and beach volleyball had soon become the norm. They played long into the summer evenings until the sun dropped from blazing high up in the sky on a canvas of electrifying blue, to hanging itself just above the waters edge, painting instead a colourful array of bright warm patterns. Sunset often signalled a barbeque at one of the family homes, where the fun and frolics would continue, until the sky turned black, and the sun was replaced by the moon. It shone brightly, high in the sky amongst an array of stars, the sea as its mirror, showing its magical reflection. There were many stories and memories shared as the pair of them had grown up together, now both at thirteen years old.

Chapter 2

As Jessica reached her pure white beach home, she left the beach and the waves behind her and bounded up the stairs, two at a time until she reached the door, which was already slightly ajar. She pushed it inwards. Bouncing straight into the living room, she was met with two petrified looking ladies staring back at her. One was her mum and the other, Blake's mum Katrina.

"Sorry!" Jessica exclaimed in a bubbly tone, trying to lighten the moment, "I didn't mean to frighten you, I was just excited to get home and see....."
Before Jessica could finish her sentence, her mum intervened in a calm but stern voice, in a way that signalled to Jessica straight away that there was a problem.
"Jessica, there is something we have to tell you. I think you should come and sit down."
There was instantly an atmosphere in the room, which Jessica didn't like the feel of. She could feel a lump developing in her throat, and her heart rate began to speed up. Her mum's face showed a very serious look now that left Jessica feeling confused. The chill in the air felt almost as though there could be something sinister in force.

Jessica followed, walking timidly, as her mum motioned for her to sit on the cream sofa that was positioned in front of the large window.
"What's happened mum?" Jessica asked, unable to bear the lingering suspense much longer, "Is something wrong?" Jessica knew that there was, from the way her mum was behaving.

Some Souls Live Forever

"Jessica....." her mum began. She was kneeling on the soft cream rug lying over the wooden floorboards, with both her hands positioned on Jessica's knees, who was now sat on the cream sofa. She was looking deep into Jessica's eyes. Jessica could see the sadness in her mum's eyes, and the red marks from where it looked as if she had been recently crying. She felt uneasy, nervous. "There's some very tragic news I have to break to you, and there is no easy way to say this." Her mum cleared her throat and paused. Although this was only for a mere few seconds, every one of those seconds seemed like eternity, and Jessica became desperate to find out what had happened.

"There has been a tragic accident", her mum began. "It happened two weeks ago, whilst we were away travelling." Jessica's mum paused again, and then began hesitantly, "Blake was taken away from us. He was knocked down by a lorry, whilst he was crossing the road, and he hit his head. He fell asleep and.....well.....he didn't ever wake up...."
Jessica searched deep into her mum's brown eyes for a different story to be told, but she couldn't find it.

"No! No!" Jessica cried in disbelief. She couldn't bear to hear the words spoken from her mother's lips. Shaking her head, she stood up and cried out, "I don't believe it! I don't believe it! What, you mean Blake is dead?"
Her mother tried to stay calm, looking at her with sympathetic eyes, "I'm sorry Jessica, I know it's hard to take this in, he has been taken to another place...."
As Jessica heard the same story repeated to her, it was almost as though her mother's voice became an echo, her words trailing off into the distance.

She looked at her mother who sat with a painful look on her face, not bearing to see the distress of her daughter who tried to comprehend what had happened. Jessica's gaze followed across the room, looking for someone to tell her this was all wrong, and that Blake would be bounding in the door any minute, like she had just done. Her gaze stopped on Katrina, Blake's mum, who sat opposite her in silence with tears streaming down her face. When Jessica's gaze met with hers, Katrina motioned to speak, but no words came out. She shook her head instead, signalling it was all much too much for her.

For a few moments, all three sat in the room quietly, whilst Jessica tried to absorb what had happened. She felt like her heart had been ripped out from her chest and torn into pieces. She couldn't bear it. She wanted this to all be wrong. Her mum moved the hair from Jessica's face and rested a firm hand on her shoulder.
"Jessica, Blake died not knowing much, the impact from the lorry was enough to take him away from us instantly. That doesn't make it feel any easier for us, but at least we know that he was not suffering for long."
Jessica didn't want to hear it. She knew her mum was only trying to help, but she just couldn't cope with the angry thoughts of disbelief she now had.

Jessica could not do or say anything. The upset felt too unbearable. She felt a burning sensation in her eyes from not blinking for a long time, letting the tears well up in her eyes so much until the point she was forced to blink and release a warm trickle of tears that rolled down her cheeks. Her mum tried hard to comfort her, by stroking her satin blond hair. There were several moments of silence as both mums sat and watched Jessica grappling to come terms with the news. Finally Jessica's mum broke the silence, "Listen, honey," her mum said in a soft voice, "No one knows how you are feeling right now, no-one can tell you what to do either.

You are in shock sweetheart. I'm going to get you a drink of peppermint tea. Is there anything you would like to know?"

Jessica sniffed. Warm tears still rolled down her face in a constant stream that seemed to have no end. There were lots of questions she wanted to ask – When it happened? Where? Why? Who did it? Where was Blake now? Although every time she tried to stop crying and ask the question, her bottom eyelids would gather with more tears and she felt so moved, she could not speak, almost as though someone had stolen her voice from inside her. She angrily pulled a tissue from box on the glass table positioned adjacent to the sofa. Dabbing away the tears, she felt the anger at the realisation that this had happened two weeks ago. It felt like electricity was suddenly running through her veins.

"So why is it that I only know about this now?" Jessica blurted out, "If Blake died two weeks ago, then I should know. Why didn't anyone tell me?" Jessica demanded answers from her mother.

"Jessica" her mum said with a hint of sternness in her voice, "You know we only ever do what we think is right," Her voice softened as she looked at Jessica's red blotchy face, obviously feeling maternal pangs at seeing the sadness of her daughter, "Katrina told me this morning that she knew what with your dad's exhibitions lasting until yesterday, there was no way we could have returned home any earlier, so she decided it was best to wait until we got home. There was no point in upsetting us whilst we were away. You would have only wanted to come home, and you know that wasn't possible what with your dad having an exhibition in Rome dedicated solely to his work only yesterday. He couldn't have cancelled it sweetheart, you know that!"

Jessica still felt the burning anger inside, which felt as though it was growing each second. As much as she understood the reasons why, Blake was her best friend and she didn't think it was right she had to hear the news two weeks after it had happened. She wanted to shout and scream, but she knew that it wasn't the right thing to do, and Jessica always tried to make the right decisions with whatever she had to do. She chose to let the feelings remain inside her, as difficult as it was.

Jessica's mum read her mind, like she always could do, "I know you must be feeling very angry and upset, and like I told you, there is nothing that anyone can say to take that away. Blake was a very special friend to you, and a fantastic person who we all loved. We will all miss him Jessica. Being angry is a perfectly normal emotion to feel right now. It's important that you give yourself some time to let your body deal with the shock. Let me get you some peppermint tea."

Jessica's mum, Anna was a teacher. She was used to handling situations like this all the time. It was natural for her to be the calming influence on the situation, and to say what needed to be said. Jessica knew her mum was right. She did feel shocked. She felt all sorts of things - shocked, angry, confused and devastated. It was like she was strapped on to an emotional rollercoaster and she could do nothing but hold on and hope the ride would soon finish, so she could step off and things would be clearer.

Jessica looked out at the sea, which still remained calm. She wished it all wasn't true. Tears continued to stream down her face, so much so, that Jessica felt there soon couldn't be any tears left in her eyes. Katrina had moved from where she had been sitting and now positioned herself on the sofa next to Jessica, reaching out to hold her hand.

"Jessica, we have arranged a special service for Blake, to be held tomorrow. We have left a slot for you to choose a special song that you would like to be played, and you could also read a poem, or tell a story if you like. I'll leave that with you. Your mum can call me later to let me know what you decide." Jessica nodded, but in reality, she couldn't really cope with the news, let alone there being a funeral the next day. It was too soon. She tried not to let her emotions overcome her in front of Katrina.

Jessica felt the warmth of Katrina's body as she leaned forward to give her a hug. Jessica returned the gesture, and held Katrina for a few moments, not wanting to let go. She felt there was lots she wanted to say, but now was not the time.

As Katrina pulled away, she took both of Jessica's hands in hers and looking deep into her eyes. "My Blake loved you Jessica. You are a very special girl to our family. Please promise me that you will take care. Give yourself time to deal with this. Jessica could see that Katrina was trying with all her might to be strong, but it was all a façade. She was truly heartbroken, just as Jessica was and Jessica could see that, no matter how hard Katrina tried to hide it.

Anna returned to the room carrying a steaming mug of peppermint tea, and a bag of frosted chocolates. She rested them carefully on the glass table, just as Katrina stood up, looking at Anna.
"I must go." Katrina said, "I have told Jessica that she can choose a song for Blake's special service tomorrow,

or anything that she would like to be read in church. Don't worry about letting me know until this evening."

Anna and Katrina embraced, and patted each other on the back, before Katrina picked up her handbag and then, rather promptly walked towards the door, as if she was trying to pull herself together and leave before she broke down again. "Take care Jessica. Love you!" Katrina said, smiling at Jessica, who forced a weak smile. Katrina pulled the door in towards her, sending a fresh sea breeze into the room. In a few moments she had gone and the door had been shut. Just as the door had been shut on the dreams that Blake and Jessica had planned to live together.

Jessica's mum had sat down next to her. In all that time, Jessica had sat with her eyes fixated on one spot on the rug, like she was transfixed in a daze. She could no longer absorb what else was going on around her. Her mum picked up the peppermint tea and handed it to Jessica, who sat clutching the steaming hot mug, positioned on her lap. They both didn't speak a word to each other, but Jessica could feel her mum's hand on her back, rubbing and comforting her. Jessica rested her head on her mum's shoulder and tried to get some comfort from the bitter sadness she felt inside.

Chapter 3

The rest of the day passed in a dream. Jessica had attempted dinner, bathed, and got into bed, trying to feel the comfort of home again after her travels, but everything had been done with her feeling as though she was present in body but not in mind. Her mind was focused on Blake, on trying to comprehend the fact that she wouldn't see him again, that he would really be gone forever. It didn't seem real yet. She half expected him to come and throw stones at her window like he used to, to wake her so that they could sneak out and sit on the beach, watching the moon's beams dance on the water and laugh about whatever antics they had gotten up to at school that day.

That wouldn't happen again and it just seemed so surreal that Jessica could not allow the thought to enter her head for long.

Exhausted from the emotional toll that the devastating news had taken on her, she fell deeply asleep nearly as soon as her head hit the pillow. Only in the morning did her eyes open again, when the sun's beams filtered their way through her curtains to wake her up.

Feeling the comfort of her bed sheets on her skin, her mind became filled with hope, "I'm home! At last I can see....." For a few microscopic milliseconds it wasn't true. Blake was still alive in her mind. But then, like a gun's bullet had hit her in the middle of her chest, and shattered the happiness into pieces, the shock of the news dawned on her, all of a sudden. She couldn't see Blake. He wasn't there to be seen, and today was the day when she would have to say goodbye to him.

Though the crack in her bedroom door, Jessica could see through to the living room, where her mum was dressed in her pure white fluffy dressing gown, sitting on the carpet, stretching as she always did in the morning, The T.V. was on in front of her and curtains open setting her alight with a pure light from the full beams of the sun reaching through the window. The sunshine lit up her face making her look almost angelic, as she sat on the floor, legs outstretched and eyes closed, reaching up to the ceiling.

Jessica sat up in bed, feeling aches all over her body, and as though all her muscles weighed like lead. She struggled to get herself out of bed and out into the living room. As soon as she opened the door, her mum stopped and quickly got to her feet, with arms outstretched to meet Jessica. She said nothing, but embraced her daughter and pulled her close.

"What time is the service?" Jessica asked, pulling away from her mum to look at her.
Her mum stroked her hair away from her face, "It's at 12pm sweetie, we need to leave at 11 so we can get there early."
"Right," Jessica said, swallowing with an uncomfortable feeling, but trying to force herself to be strong. "I'd better get ready then. What time is it?" she asked.
"Its 10 now, you have time", she paused, but Jessica said nothing, "I told Katrina about the song you wanted, it was 'More than words' is that right?"

"Yes…" Jessica returned with sadness in her voice, her sentence trailing off at the end. She wanted to be more helpful to her mum, to give more of a response as her mum had done nothing but be supportive, but she just couldn't summon the energy. It was as if someone had sucked all of the energy out of her and she was struggling, like she was walking through thick mud and getting no-where fast.

Jessica walked into the kitchen, in an almost 'zombie-like' state. Walking straight over to the refrigerator, she pulled the door towards her which felt far heavier than it usually did. Jessica stood at the refrigerator motionless, trying to make a decision. She must have stood there for several minutes, just with the door open, doing nothing, because soon, Jessica felt goose pimples all over her upper body. Trying hard to snap into reality, she grabbed the tub of margarine from the top shelf. Slamming the door shut, Jessica walked over to the bread bin and pulled out the first two pieces of bread she laid her hands on. She lit the grill and put the bread in ready to toast.

"This is crazy!" Jessica said out loud. "Where are you Blake?" Jessica asked, for some reason looking up at the ceiling. "You can't be dead, this is crazy!" Jessica said, again talking to the white patchy ceiling, expecting it would summon an answer. She poured a cup of tea from the already steaming teapot that sat on the sideboard, and pulled the sugar jar towards her. Taking the spoon that her mum had already used, left stranded on the draining board, Jessica pulled the sugar pot lid off with force and plonked it down on the sideboard heavily. She began spooning the sugar into her tea. Jessica normally didn't drink any sugar, but today she put four heaped teaspoons into her steaming hot tea. It seemed the right thing to do.

As Jessica watched the water spin as she stirred her tea, moving the spoon quickly in circles, trying hard to make the water spin in a whirlpool, she found herself realising there was a smell of smoke filling the air. Taking a few deeper breaths, to check if her senses were correct, Jessica quickly sprang out of her dazed state and yanked the bread out from the toaster. The top of the two pieces of bread were completely charred black, with smoke bellowing from them. Without a moment's hesitation, Jessica tossed the toast into the sink, and swivelled the cold tap onto full burst, sending clouds of steam into the kitchen.

It wasn't long before Jessica could hear the piercing sound of the smoke alarm breaking the quietness of the morning. Jessica's mum soon came bounding into the kitchen, screaming at a level to make her voice heard over the sound of the alarm,
"What's happened?" she asked, spotting the charcoaled toast sat on the grill pan in the sink. Jessica turned to look at her mum, but didn't show any emotion on her face at all. "Come here!" Jessica's mum continued, pulling her daughter by the arm, so that she could hug her. Jessica nestled herself onto her mum's shoulder, smelling the scent of her perfume. It gave her some comfort, despite the noise of the alarm, which still continued to sound.

This wasn't like Jessica. She was efficient and quick, and normally very calm. She told herself this as she stepped into the shower. Her mum had offered to make breakfast, as she and Jessica and both realised that the shock had taken its toll on Jessica, and she felt incapable of doing very much at all.

Chapter 4

Soon it was time to leave for the funeral. As Jessica walked down the steps of her house and towards the white car that would take them to the service, she found herself repeatedly telling herself to be calm in an attempt to keep it together. She could feel the sweat on her palms and her heart racing in her chest, as she thought about the prospect of the day ahead. As the car pulled away, Jessica felt sick with nerves. She wished so desperately that this could be so different. She tried hard to prevent herself from crying, as she clutched her hands together. The feel of the black leather seats sticking to her skin, distressing her slightly, contrasted with the feel of the air conditioning on her face which felt refreshing. It didn't seem real. None of it seemed true. How could she be going to her best friend's funeral? Why was this happening?

Soon, the car pulled up outside St Swithun's church. Jessica could see people communing outside the large church doors which were swung wide open. Waves of people dressed in black swept into the church. Jessica spotted faces she hadn't seen in months, waiting to file into the hall. Blake's aunties and uncles, school friends, his favourite granddad sporting a new wheelchair and with his grey hair slicked back as always. There was a mixed reaction from all, some looking distraught with faces drawn and pale, others somehow summoning a smile. All were in the same place now for the same reason. To say goodbye to Blake.

Jessica stepped out of the door that her dad had opened for her. He smiled at her from beneath his moustache, his bright blue eyes gazing into hers with affection. Jessica loved her dad. He was her rock in life.

No matter what happened, everything was ok when he was there to comfort her. When he was in the room with her, she felt safe. She knew she was going to need him today. Taking him by the arm, she felt her nerves ease slightly, as she made her way into the church.

As Jessica felt the warmth of the sunshine disappear inside the church, goose pimples stood up on their ends all over her arms. Glorious sounds of church music filled the air and the floral scent of the flowers hit her as soon as Jessica entered the candle filled room. Inside, row upon row of black dressed figures sat looking forward at an empty space where soon a coffin would lay. It was surrounded by a beautiful array of flowers and wreaths.

Jessica felt awkward inside the church. It felt almost as though she was not in control of her body. Her legs were moving, but she was just following her dad's lead, who took her by the arm and walked her forward to the front row. She sat on the stiff wooden chair next to where Katrina would sit. Looking forward at the flowers, her eyes soon focused upon a wreath that spelled "Blake" which caused an instant sickness in her belly to overcome her, so much so, she thought she was going to faint. Squeezing her dad's hands, she clenched her teeth together and tried to hold it together, though it seemed all too much for her to bear.

Soon everyone was seated. The scurrying stopped and the talking ceased. There was a few a moments of silence, which meant the only thing Jessica could hear was the ever racing beat of her heart in her ear drums. Soon Blake's favourite song, the one she had chosen began to fill the church, and the back doors of the church were opened. Jessica focused her eyes on the front of the church, not bearing to see the coffin being carried. "It can't be him!" her mind kept telling her, "this can't be real." She felt her dad's hand squeeze hers gently.

Out the corner of her eye, Jessica saw the wooden coffin being carried by black suited men walking in perfect timing with each other.

Jessica had tried hard to fight the tears all day, but she couldn't stop them from falling any longer. Suddenly, streams came flooding, as she felt the sadness overcome her. She squeezed her dad's hand again tightly. It felt like a knot in her stomach was twisting. Her heart was pounding so quickly that she could actually feel the blood from each heartbeat pounding against her chest. She tasted the salt on her lips as the tears trickled down to her mouth.

The coffin was laid to rest in its special place in the church, next to the flowers that spelled Blake's name. Those who had followed the coffin moved to their places. Katrina took her place next to Jessica, and Jessica's mum next to Katrina, both of them holding hands. Soon everyone was seated and the vicar began speaking.

Chapter 5

Much of the service passed in a blur. Jessica felt as if she was in a distant land, not totally in touch with what was going on around her. The vicar's condolences and prayers had passed over her in a haze, as her mind was more focused on her own thoughts. Swimming round and round in her head were thoughts of denial, thinking that this couldn't possibly be happening, and that the coffin lay in front of the church couldn't possibly be Blake. He was too fit and healthy to be laying there in the wooden encasing. She half imagined that at any minute, as she had done when she had first heard the news, that he would come bounding in, through the back doors, revealing this was all some disturbed dream.

Throughout the service, Jessica had glanced over at her family around her several times to check for people's reactions, seeing on their faces the mirrored distress that she felt. In those moments in the service, when she had felt like she couldn't cope, she had tried hard to focus on the beautiful flowers surrounding the coffin, or the brightness of the stain glassed windows, displaying pictures of Jesus with his disciples.

When the song that she had chosen played for the second time, in a moment of reflection, Jessica truly felt a desperate aching for Blake, almost as though someone had their hands clenched around her heart, squeezing the life out of it. She had remembered the many times they had sung this song at the tops of their voices. It had been a song they had played to cheer them up, a song for when one of them was scared, a song for happy times too when they wanted to celebrate. As the strong beats of the drums and enigmatic sounds of the heavy guitar music had filled her ears, she had pictured Blake vividly. His enchanting blue eyes that were set deep in his face, his gorgeous brown hair and chisel like jaw, now came to her thoughts again, as she remembered the last time she had seen him. It had been just before Jessica had left, bound for Italy with her family. She could picture his friendly smile beaming at her, as he wrapped his arms around her waist and lifted her into the air, swinging her around in a circle. She remembered how much she had squealed at his tickling touch and how that had nearly caused him to drop her, because he always couldn't bear Jessica's high pitched screams.

When it was time to say the last goodbye to Blake, gentle music filled the church, where no man or women stood with a dry eye, as they reflected for a while, thinking about Blake or saying their own special prayers. Jessica had glanced at her mum and Katrina, who still sat holding hands, leaning in towards each other, with shoulders stooped over, trying hard to provide some comfort for each other. Jessica was sure she could see the bones in her mum's hand; the frail skin that covered them was stretched tightly as she held Katrina's hand. Her dad was sat bolt upright, not crying, but with tears gathered in his eye lids, his mouth slightly down turned at the edges, beneath his moustache. Jessica hated seeing people upset. She was a girl who survived through seeing people happy, through enjoying making people smile and laugh as often as she could. It wasn't right that she saw the grief displayed on everyone's faces.

Jessica watched in a blurry haze from the tears that had fallen, the suited men walking towards the coffin to carry it to its final resting place. Their black shiny boots walked exactly in the same motion, in complete time with each other, as they gracefully carried the coffin towards the back of the church, where the hearse would be waiting.

Jessica had decided not to attend the burial, as she didn't believe that Blake would be buried in the ground. She knew, deep inside her that Blake would never leave her; he would always be there, protecting her and guiding her. Right at this very moment, she reminded herself of this. Both of them had talked about this one evening several months ago, intrigued by an R.E. lesson that they had been taught at school that day. Sat outside on the veranda of her beach house sipping cool lemonade, Jessica remembered the conversation when they decided what they had believed to be true. They had watched the children from the sailing club meander in and out of the buoys, following their instructor in their mini dinghy's, with their colourful sails blowing gently in the cool breeze.

It was a special conversation, when they had both decided on that day about their true thoughts about life. Both Blake and Jessica believed that each and every person or creature possessed an inner soul that was unique and special. They had decided on that day, that everyone's soul was on the earth for a reason.

They had both felt that in the journey of life, that some souls met and stayed together for a long time, entwined, and dancing together all of their lives, set to always influence each other and share what life had to offer. Others met only for a short while before parting again and continuing on their own journey, but nevertheless sometimes leaving a big mark, an impression on that person that would always be there. Almost as though it was meant to happen, to maybe change that person to help them move on a different path or to think in a different way.

Jessica wasn't sure about her belief in God, but she definitely believed in a spiritual world that helped govern everything. What she couldn't understand, was why Blake's soul had to leave his body now, when there were so many reasons for him to be still alive – so many ambitions and dreams to fulfil. She knew there was an answer, but she couldn't quite understand the reasons yet.

As the service came to an end, and Jessica walked towards the back door of the church, arm in arm with her father, she realised how exhausted she felt from the emotional energy that she had used since hearing about Blake's death.

The blazing sunshine illuminated Jessica's face as she took her first step out of the church, causing her to rapidly blink. She realised the hearse had thankfully departed, and she was now met with swarms of people dressed in black, gathered talking.

Jessica spotted two grey haired ladies waddling over towards her with drawn faces displaying their empathy.
"How are you darling?" one of the ladies asked inquisitively. Jessica realised it was one of her neighbours peering at her inquisitively over her red spectacles, "I'm sorry to hear of the tragic loss, he was such a sweetie. I watched you two running around on the sand since you were knee high, and I've seen you grow up together over all those years."

Jessica instantly felt a surprising surge of anger running through her veins. She knew the lady was merely trying to be nice, but she just didn't want to hear about the tragedy now. Jessica would never display her anger, instead simply gesturing in a friendly way, replying that she was ok, whilst inwardly wreathing.

Her dad realised her daughter's instant change in mood, a subtlety only he would be receptive to. Her arm that was interlocked with his was stroked gently by his other hand as a mark of comfort that it was ok to feel the way she did. Jessica's dad was the most amazingly astute man, who could always detect Jessica's feelings better than anyone else. He looked down at her and gave her a wink.

Before long, as the two of them managed to make their excuses and depart from the ladies, walking along towards Anna, Jessica's mum; another group of middle-aged ladies from the church wandered over. They were dressed in posh dresses, with black sunglasses and hugely oversized handbags that looked rather as though they were trying desperately hard to stay young.
"Jessica darling, how are you?" one of the taller ladies asked. One by one, they bent over and kissed both her cheeks, as though they knew her well, when really she had only met them once or twice.

"I'm fine" Jessica said, between gritted teeth.

"Oh you can't be fine darling; you don't have to lie to us. It's ok to be sad you know. That's what people expect. We know you're a strong cookie. But it's ok to share your emotions." The lady looked at Jessica with sympathetic eyes.

Jessica smiled sweetly. Inside that surge of anger returned, this time the fire in her belly a little more explosive. She hardly knew these ladies, how on earth could they tell her how she should be feeling? What did people want her to do? Fall down on her knees and burst into tears in front of everyone? Scream to the high heavens in hope that God would bring Blake back?

No. Jessica was different. She had always been known by everyone as being calm, and someone who could be strong. Blake and her always used to have private joke to themselves about how other people over-reacted to situations. They had both always dealt with things by looking for the positive aspects of every situation. It was in her nature to be that way.

Jessica tried to think of an excuse to slip away from the ladies. She found herself craving the sea desperately. She needed to feel the calm and the serenity of the waves. Everyone's plans were to head to the wake at a local restaurant, in celebration of Blake, but Jessica no longer possessed the same inner strength to go along with convention. She just couldn't do it, and right now, more than anything else, she wanted to be alone.

Jessica tugged on her father's sleeve at his elbow and stood on tip toes to whisper into his ear, "I'm going dad. I need to be alone."
Her father turned around and grabbed Jessica tightly, holding her by her arms. He bent down slightly so that his eye-line was level with hers.

"Tell me honestly Jessica. Is this what you really want?" he spoke rather seriously, and the look of concern made his face wrinkle up, and gave him a ridge on his forehead between his eyes that he always showed when he was worried. Jessica nodded, pursing her lips together and saying with child-like murmurs that made her father's heart melt, "I want to be by the sea. I don't want to go to the wake dad; I want to say my goodbyes alone."

Jessica's father didn't say anymore, as he had always believed in his daughter's ability to know that she made good decisions. His arms enveloped hers, as he pulled her tightly into his chest, before letting her go and nodding reassuringly.

Taking one final look at the church, watching the spire stretch high into the sky, as if it were piercing the clouds, Jessica took a deep sigh and turned and looked towards the sea. It was only a mile or so walk, and she craved the space and time to let her thoughts wander, without interruption.

Chapter 6

The walk passed with Jessica once again being in a trance like state, her feet simply walking one at a time, following the motions but with no thoughtful consideration. As soon as her feet touched the sand, Jessica felt an instant surge of peace throughout her body. She took a deep breath, filling her lungs with coolness from the fresh sea air. She felt, no matter how tired she was, she wanted to walk for miles into the distance and leave all her troubles behind her. Quickly, she began pacing, one foot in front of another. The force of the strong sea breeze blew her white linen shirt horizontal at the ends as she felt the stain against her body.

How dare those ladies make her feel so angry.

Jessica paced her way down to the shoreline, where the sand was wet and solid. She didn't stop to look at the sea, she just carried on walking, flip flops in hand, her arms swinging quickly.

Thoughts of the coffin lying in the church returned to her mind, but she tried desperately to block them out by focusing on the scenes in front of her. Restaurants and cafes lined the beach for several miles, with rows of sun-glassed people lounging on the chairs on the balconies, enjoying the rays.

Leaves on the trees positioned adjacent to the beach blew with such a force, that the branches wobbled two and fro, sending leaves off twisting into the air. Pieces of rubbish left strewn on the beach followed the same path, blowing into the air and along the shore, tumbling and rolling as the winds' hands lifted and dropped them.

Jessica realised the weather reflected how she too was feeling.

Suddenly, in an instant, Jessica hastily stopped in her tracks. She let herself really feel the anger that had been building for the last two days, but that she had been forced to keep inside, due to everyone around her. Like a thunderstorm was raging inside her body sending volts up and down her spinal chord, she let herself succumb to her emotions, now that everyone she knew was out of sight. With force, she threw her flip flops onto the sandy floor ahead of her, and fell to her knees, sobbing. Jessica felt all her emotions overtake her body. She clenched her fists tightly, so much so, that she dug her fingernails deep into her palms, almost causing them to bleed. Not caring about the pain, she continued to punch the sand by her sides, desperately feeling the pain that Blake was gone.

"It's not fair!" she screamed out, still punching the floor, "Why did Blake have to die? She screeched, looking up to the sky as if talking to the heavens. "Why not some other person? Why him? He was my best friend." Jessica screamed. She stopped punching the floor, and hugged her knees tightly into her chest. Jessica felt pain in her chest, deep inside her. An aching that no medicine or doctor could cure. She rolled onto her side and sobbed, completely overcome by her grief. Laying there for several moments, holding herself rigidly, Jessica cried rivers of tears.

After a while, gradually the tears stopped, as she looked out at the waves. They were crashing against the groynes and rocks violently. Sprays of white water leap up high and crashed down against the jagged rocks. Jessica thought for a moment that it was as if Blake was speaking to her through the waves, and reacting to her feelings, echoing the same anger. Jessica watched intently, using the clashes and smashes of the sea to numb her senses to how she truly felt inside.

Realising the moistness of the sand was dampening her skin, causing her to itch slightly, Jessica took a deep sigh and sat upright, looking all around her. On the beach people were everywhere. She watched for a while scanning the beach. There were all sorts of people out today. Sunbathers lay, covered in sun cream on various mats in an attempt to catch the sun's last rays of the year. Surfers scattered along the coast waited and watched for the next waves. Two older people walked gracefully together, their white skin set against their matching blue socks walking in brown flip flops, and white peaked hats positioned on their heads. Seagulls jostled two and fro in the air, swooping high in the sky above.

Jessica found her eyes focused on two dogs, playfully splashing in and out of the waves, playing chase. Her eyes followed their movements, as the spotted the spaniel lying down momentarily, whilst growling sat the collie, who ran over, ready to pounce. Just as the collie got there, paws spread in the air ready to attack, the spaniel leapt up backwards and sprinted off, barking excitedly as if laughing at the collie who was left falling to the floor. It made Jessica laugh, which then felt like such a relief. This made her feel calm again, as if all her anger had momentarily been taken away. The sounds of her laughing to herself, made her summon the energy to be able to stand to her feet and decide to walk back towards home.

Chapter 7

As Jessica walked within a few footsteps of her beachside house, she saw her mum and dad, and her older brother Darren stepping out of the taxi. As soon as she caught her brother's eye, he came bounding over to her, leaving her mum and dad to pay for the taxi. Jessica realised at that moment, she hadn't actually spoken to her brother much at all throughout the emotion of the last two days.

Darren ran over, flinging sand everywhere as his feet kicked the ground and scooped it into the air. His long blonde surfer hair bounced up and down as his body ran athletically along the warm sand.
"You ok Jess?" he said with a big smile that revealed his perfectly formed white teeth, "Been worried about you, because I haven't been around much the last couple of days what with catching up with Laura, but you know I've been thinking about you don't you?"

Laura was Darren's girlfriend. Jessica didn't really like her much. Not for any particular reason, as she was a nice girl, but there was just something between the two of them which didn't click.

"I'm ok! You know me! I don't ever like to be around people when I'm upset, I just craved the sea." Jessica said, looking up at her brother.

Darren looked out towards the sea and took a deep breath, then motioned himself to the side of Jessica and slumped his thick muscular arm around her shoulder, pulling her in towards his body. He knew exactly how much the sea meant to Jessica, as he had the same feelings. Being a surfer, he was always found out in the sea catching the waves, even early in the morning, as soon as the first gulls arose from their slumber and were heard echoing their calls as they glided through the newly lit sky, over-looking the water.

"Well, sis what do you say to catching some waves later? The sun will be up for at least another couple of hours, and looks like there are definitely some white waves out there to ride in on? What'dya say?" he asked joyfully, raising his eyebrows like a cute little puppy.

Jessica looked out to the sea, which peaked and dipped with the rolling waves. She thought to herself for a moment about whether she could be bothered to go surfing. Then the realisation came that she needed to try and create some happiness for herself, "Yea, ok!" she said, heaving a big sigh.

The prospect of surfing made Jessica think of that buzzing feeling of catching a wave just at the right moment, and feeling its push behind her. She remembered the endless energy it would always give her. Maybe that is what would do her good right now.
"Cool!" Darren said, still squeezing her shoulder tightly and leading her towards their home. "You go and get changed and I'll wax up the boards." He pitched her another of those smiles and gave her a wink, like he always did, his beaming teeth peeking out from the blonde specks of stubble sticking out all over his chin. He was just like her dad, always protective of her feelings.

Jessica gave him a tentative smile and made her way to the front steps. She felt the instant change in the temperature of the sand on her feet, as she moved from the sunshine onto the sand shaded by her house. The coldness of the grains of sand made her quicken her pace so that she ran up the blue steps two at a time.

Reaching the door, which was already half open, Jessica waltzed into the room to be met with her parents embraced in the living room holding each other closely This day had been hard for them also. Noticing her presence in the room, they pulled away from each other, both looking at Jessica with the same expression of wanting to protect her innocence.

"Darren has asked me to go surfing with him. I figured I should probably go." Jessica said, trying hard to summon a smile, causing her dad to beam a big smile back at her, and her mum's face to soften a little. This made Jessica smile just a little more, despite how she felt about Blake, as it made her realise how much they cared for her.

"I'll just go and get my wetsuit on." Darren said "The sun will be out for a couple of hours, and then we'll come in." Jessica felt the energy returning to her body as she thought again about surfing.

"Well, I thought fish and chips tonight, so whenever you fancy eating, we can nip down to Ramie's. Good idea gorgeous?" her mum said, glad to see that Jessica was feeling a little more in control again.

"Great!" Jessica replied, her mouth watering instantly at the prospect of her soon being able to devour her favourite junk food. She had only been able to eat a single slice of toast in the last 24 hours, so by now she was starting to feel the pangs of hunger again. She walked towards her room to find her favourite blue wetsuit. It felt as though she was smiling a little smile inside, reacting to the love her family had shown, and knowing she was cared for.

Some Souls Live Forever

Quickly rummaging through her laundry, she pulled out by one of the feet, her blue neoprene wetsuit. Turning to face the mirror, Jessica caught her own eye, noticing her blond ringlets hung loosely around her shoulders, which showed her golden tan partially hidden beneath her white linen shirt. As she stepped nearer to the mirror, and looked closely, Jessica noticed the dark circles beneath her blue eyes. Her finger moved to her left eye and brushed beneath it gently, trying to put some colour back into the skin which looked wragged. She moved her finger down to brush her cheeks, which had slightly caught the sun and looked a little shiny. Her finger stopped on her cheek for an instant as she realised just how much her life was going to change now that Blake was no longer around.

As this thought entered her mind, she pulled away from the mirror in a second trying to dispel it from her and focus back on the few moments of positivity she had experienced since meeting Darren. She hastily grabbed her wetsuit and cuddled it in towards her chest. Remembering her brother was outside greasing the boards, Jessica decided to dismiss her thoughts of Blake, and try to focus on surfing. Quickly, she unchanged and squeezed her limbs into the tight neoprene. Pulling the zip behind her to encase her completely, she took one last glance in the mirror and gently ran out of her bedroom door, through the living room and down the steps, back into the coolness of breeze on this summer afternoon.

Darren was already out in the sea, lying on his board like a tiger waiting for it's prey. He lay lingering in front of the white ripples of the break in the sea. He was looking over his shoulder, ready to pounce at any moment. Jessica decided to collect her board and go and join him. Her eyes caught sight of her board which lay down on the sand beside their hut, smooth and glistening in the evening sun, as if it was brand new. Jessica lifted up the board, and quickly ran out to join her brother.

Not stopping as she hit the sea, Jessica felt the boundless energy fill her, as she lifted her knees high and ran out to into the deeper water. As she wriggled into the sea at waist level, she heard her brother screaming at the top of his lungs,
"What a beauty!"
Instantly catching Jessica's attention, she watched her brothers athletic frame spring to his feet on his board, just at the break was a metre behind him. Looking cool and completely in control, he casually glided in on the board directly into the shore, as if the seas strong hands were pushing his board all the way. Within a few metres of the beach, his board wobbled slightly, sending his arms in a propeller like motion as if trying to grab hold of the air, which had no handles to hold.

It tickled Jessica, and she laughed loudly, before springing onto her own board, and swimming out towards the break. She tasted the salt of the sea as it splashed over the edges of her board and onto her face. She didn't care. Not having to stay motionless there for long, as a huge wave came tumbling in towards her. Watching carefully for the correct moment, Jessica waited patiently, and then jumped onto her knees and felt the powerful push behind her. As the pace quickened and the board was steadily balanced, she jumped forward onto her feet and held her arms out to balance herself.

Closing her eyes, Jessica felt the wind against her face and the push of the board beneath her feet, which felt like complete freedom. Taking a deep breath to fill her lungs and holding her arms outstretched, she glided for as long as she could, before feeling the wobble as the board met shallow water. She jumped onto the gravel beneath her, and desperate to feel that same feeling again, she quickly grabbed her board and sprinted out towards the break, this time to see if she could catch the same wave as her brother, who was already out at waist level, looking out hopefully for his next target.

Jessica waded out to join him. Both of them lay there on their boards for several moments looking out to horizon which displayed deep shades of oranges and reds.
"You ok Jessie?" Darren shouted out to her, but not moving his gaze from the waves.
"Yeah, great!" she returned, this time not having to force it, but actually feeling really great, forgetting everything that upset her.
"Here we go Jessie, get ready! Big one coming!" her brother shouted over the sound of the crashes and splashes of the wave rolling towards them.

It was a big one too! Several feet high this time, but Jessica was ready to take it on! Both surfers turned around to face the shore line, and watched patiently over their shoulder, ready for that moment when…
"Go!" her brother shouted, "paddle Jessie!"

Both of them tugged at the sea with their arms, pulling through the water, their arms circling like Olympic cyclists racing for gold. As soon as the wave reached within several inches of them; both of them leapt simultaneously, with athletic grace, from their knees straight onto their feet, feeling the force propelling them along the fresh blue sea.

Jessica couldn't help but smile. A smile that made her face stretch, and a buzzing energy filled the whole of her body. She kept her eyes open this time, catching a glimpse of her brother to the side of her. She daren't turn around to look in case she lost her balance. Looking along to her beach house in front of her, Jessica looked at the top window, where the curtains had been drawn and peeping out from between them was her mum, waving enthusiastically.

"Look Darren, its mum!" Jessica shouted, waving frantically back. Jessica waited for a reply, but couldn't hear one. Reaching the shallow shore, Jessica looked over her side to watch Darren, but he wasn't with her at the shore line. She glanced back at the sea, feeling a surge of nervousness running through her, to see Darren's board floating, but no Darren.

Jessica hastily un-velcroed her board from her ankle and began running out to the sea. Her heart was racing, and her mind desperately alternating between thoughts of hoping he was not injured or worse, and thoughts of calmness, telling herself everything was going to be ok. Thankfully, after merely taking a few steps, Jessica stopped as she saw Darren pop his head up from the sea line, rearing his head by the side of his board. Jessica stopped in her tracks and breathed a sigh of relief, cursing herself beneath her breath for being so silly. It wasn't like her to become so worried. Her and her brother had been surfing ever since they were very young, when they first learnt to swim. Jessica, feeling the surge of adrenaline subside replaced by tiredness, turned back to face the beach and began walking in towards her board. Her brother followed.

As she reached the beach, Jessica plonked herself down in the sand, pulling her knees into her chest and

rocking her body slightly to keep her warm. She watched Darren leave the sea behind him and exit to join her.
"You ok sis? My watch came off; I had to dive in to get it! Lucky I found it eh?" he said, showing her his find. "I reckon a couple more waves and then we'll have to go in."

Jessica turned to face her brother and smiled a gentle smile, "I'm ok. You go, and I will stay and watch!"
She saw her brother's eye brows tense forming a crinkle on his forehead between his eyes, the same look that their father had when he was concerned, "You serious?" he asked.

"Yes, honestly, I'm happy don't worry, just want to watch and learn from the master!" she said, smiling up at him. Darren smiled back at her.

"You know its true little lady!" he said, jumping to his feet and running out to his board taking to the challenge. She watched his blonde hair swing from side to side and he lunged out towards the sea.

Jessica found herself thinking about Blake again. It had been at least half an hour, and that was probably the longest time she had spent without him entering her thoughts.

Now, Jessica found herself thinking again about Blake's soul. She thought again about what Blake and her had decided in that conversation not so long ago, the belief that every soul would complete a journey in life, that it had a purpose for being alive, and only when it had fulfilled that purpose, would it be taken to a higher place. She still couldn't make any sense of why Blake's soul was taken so early then as he had so much more to offer the world, and so much more to enjoy in the world himself. She just couldn't comprehend why this had happened so early on in his life.

Jessica watched Darren glide into the shore from his last wave. He picked up both of their boards, ready to go in for the night. Jessica suddenly remembered that school started again the next day, which she would need strength for, so now was time for fish and chips.

Chapter 8

It wasn't like Jessica to take a day off school. In fact, thinking about it, Jessica couldn't recollect a single day when she had taken a day off school on purpose. Normally being a bubbly person who always made the most of her life, she didn't really ever feel the need to stay at home. She always liked being around people, and especially being around her best buddy Blake.

Today was different. There was absolutely no way Jessica was going to school. The last few days had passed in a whirlwind. Everything had happened so quickly, that Jessica felt almost physically sick as she remembered all the events. There was no way she could even contemplate school today. It was totally out of the question.

Jessica had decided this at 2am in the morning. Finding herself wide awake for most of the night, peering out through the crack in the curtains to look at the stars shining like mini lanterns in the jet black sky, Jessica had wondered if Blake was one of the stars looking back at her. She had talked to him and told him that she loved him, and missed him. She tried to think of what he would say back to her, maybe he would tell her he loved her too and missed her. Thinking this and picturing his face each time she closed her eyes made it all a little too distressing. She tried so hard to cut out the images of Blake from her mind so that she could get some sleep, but after several hours of doing this, and feeling terribly frustrated, Jessica decided she needed the next day to herself.

When the alarm had sounded in the morning, Jessica had pounced on the off button with her hand, like a cat catching a mouse, which sent the alarm flying onto the ground. She had then turned over, facing her back to where the alarm clock had been placed, and feeling heavy eyed, fallen straight back to sleep.

Jessica's mum and dad and her brother Darren had obviously decided too that Jessica needed some extra sleep, because normally one of them could be relied upon to be the second wake up call, for those mornings when the alarm clock was not really enough to summon a response from her.

It was 11.30am when Jessica finally decided to open her eyes to start the day. She lay in bed and pondered for a while, thinking about what she was going to do that day. This didn't last long, because Jessica soon felt a dryness in her mouth causing her to move to get a cold glass of juice from the kitchen. Walking into the living room, Jessica realised she was alone. Her house was mainly open-plan with only very few walls to divide the house into its parts, so she instantly could tell there was no-one else with her, unless in the bedrooms.

"Mum?... Dad?... Darren?..." Jessica called out. No response. She was definitely by herself. She noticed a note hung on the fridge. It read "Call me if you need me. Mum x"

Jessica walked over to the fridge door and opened it towards her, casting a yellow glow of light onto her face, and a waft of cool air refreshing and calming on her skin. Jessica reached for the milk bottle, and clasping it by its frosty milk top, she pulled it towards her chest, holding it there for a little while to feel the chill against her skin. Taking an upturned glass from the draining board, she poured herself a tall glass of fresh milk. As soon as she put the milk bottle down, Jessica took the glass to her lips and began to gulp the milk quickly without drawing breath, as though she hadn't had a drink at all in several days. Finishing the glass, she slammed it back onto the counter and stood there for a while, staring at the wooden floor in a dreamy state.

She thought of what she could do with the day. Staying in bed was not an option, nor staying in the house. It felt empty and lonely. She considered surfing, but decided she didn't really have the energy to do this. Perhaps she could go into town for a wander. Maybe the hustle and bustle of people roaming around would be good for her, and she really wanted to see Darren who worked in a surf shop there. He was the one person who had really helped her feel better, and right now, she needed to be close to him.

Casting her eyes out towards the sea line from the front room window, Jessica found herself slumping herself down on the sofa. Her eyes stayed there for a moment, watching the ripples of the sea as she always did. That view was like her tranquiliser, and every time she stared at it, it was almost as though she became drunk by staring at its beauty, totally mesmerised and captivated. It was another beautiful day. The sun was already shining high in the azure blue sky with no clouds anywhere to taint the view.

After several more moments watching, Jessica moved into her bedroom and tugged at her pile of freshly clean clothes. There she found her favourite pair of pale blue jogging bottoms and her white hoodie. She decided not to take a shower today, not really caring much for her appearance. Catching a glimpse of herself in the mirror made her realise how drab and dreary she looked, her skin almost grey and sickly. Her blond hair that once hung in beautiful glossy ringlets now looked a tattered matt of dry coarseness. She didn't even bother to try and detangle and put the shine back into it, a simple loose band around it would suffice for today.

Jessica decided she was going to catch the bus into town. Making her way out of the house, Jessica slammed the door shut behind her and walked down the stairs out towards the bus stop. It wasn't far from her house. In five minutes she would be there. It was quiet outside. Apart from the older couple that Jessica spotted walking away from her down the street, Jessica was almost alone. She didn't like it. Although she wanted the day to herself, she still wanted to be around people.

It wasn't long before the big yellow bus that rode into town pulled up at the bus stop. Inside a friendly looking man with a red baseball cap perched on his head sat at the drivers seat, greeting her with a beaming smile. Jessica tried to summon a smile back, but her attempts were feeble.

"Come on lady!" the bus driver exclaimed, "Give us a smile! What's wrong? Someone died?"

Jessica felt a sword being thrust through her heart. She refrained from lashing out at the driver, and instead placed her payment into his hand with a little force, and without saying a word, walked instantly towards a spare seat, gritting her teeth to keep her anger at his comment inside. As she walked away from the driver, she heard him mutter under his breath something about people being rude around these parts. Jessica, finding this totally unbelievable, kept walking towards her seat. There were plenty to choose from, as only a man wearing headphones with his hoodie top up over his head, which was moving to the beat of his music, was there to keep her company. Jessica flung herself down on the red fabric seats and tried to think about where she was going to go in town. Jessica thought about how ignorant the bus driver was to say such a stupid thing.

As the bus roared its engines and pulled away from the curb, Jessica looked out the window and watched the world pass by. Thankfully, the journey into town was only ten minutes or so away because she felt the urge to be moving and walking, and her belly began to rumble with an insatiable hunger.

Chapter 9

The bus ride jolted Jessica two and fro, almost as though the bus driver was displaying his emotions through his driving. Jessica was sure he was driving with extra speed over the bumps and around the corners because he was annoyed. Jessica had watched the passers by, wondering what they were doing with their days, where they were going and who they would be meeting. As the bus drove nearer into town, the number of people Jessica could watch grew. Even though it was a weekday, still swarms of people filtered in and out of the city streets carrying bags. Cyclists filtered in and out of the traffic which mostly stayed stationary due to the volume moving into town. Jessica watched a lady who looked to be in her twenties with two young children holding onto her hands. All three skipped along the street together, singing away without a care in the world. Jessica wanted to be that lady. How lovely it would be to have her own little people to look after and to sing along with.

As the bus jolted to a halt, Jessica was nearly flung off her seat. She felt nervous having to exit off the bus, worried about what the driver may say to her as she passed by him. She looked down at the floor as she walked at a quick pace, desperate to leave the bus as quickly as she could. Thankfully the bus driver did not even try to acknowledge her. Little did he know that he has made such an error on first greeting her, that right now, she could not forgive.

Jessica smelt the fumes from the bus as its exhaust sent clouds of grey burning smut into the air, and passing cars also polluted the city. What a vast difference to the clean smells of the beach. Jessica waited for the right moment to cross the street, finding a gap between two cars, she dashed across the road. Her insatiable appetite reminded her that she needed food, as her stomach rumbled as a signal for food. Weaving in and out of people, Jessica made her way to the nearest bakery. There at the clear glass window she stood and looked at the array of delicacies, trying to decide which one she wanted most.

Glazed donuts were her favourites, but today she wanted something really sugary with whipped cream. She decided on an extra large chocolate éclair. Feeling her mouth begin to water at the prospect of the delicious taste in her mouth, she quickly made her way into the shop. The old lady at the counter had a warmth about her, a certain aura that gave the sense that the lady was a really kind and gentle person.

In front of her was a glass cabinet, filled with bakery goods. Row upon row of deserts sat in lines next to each other. Jessica stared for a while at the assortment of strawberry cheesecakes, chocolate donuts, cream tarts and gingerbread men, not to mention sugary donuts and extra large fondant fancies. An array of delicious smelling breads sat next to the deserts, some twisted in plaits, others topped with melted cheese. The smell was irresistible.

"How can I help you dear?" the lady asked, with a softness to her voice. Jessica thought she looked such a sweet person, with the odd strand of curly grey hair poking out from beneath her white hat and friendly blue eyes that could light up anyone's day.
"A chocolate éclair please!" Jessica asked timidly, pointing to the cabinet where the freshly whipped cream éclairs lay. She tried to summon a smile, but the

muscles on her face felt tight from the tears she had wept in the days gone by.

"Just the one my dear? Is there anything else I can do for you?" the lady asked gently.

Jessica wished she could. She thought to herself she wished she could ask the lady to make all of what had happened a dream.

"No, thank you!" Jessica replied, this time managing a smile, as she took the white paper bag from the lady and handed over her change. The lady had such a warm and friendly face, like a grandma that everyone wished they could have.

Jessica walked out of the bakery and watched the sights of the town, where cars whizzed by at speed, and flocks of people moved in and out of shops. Not having any real intention to go anywhere special, she decided to walk up the high-street towards the town centre.

Pulling her éclair from the bag and taking her first bite, Jessica instantly felt even calmer for tasting the rich chocolate sauce that oozed into her mouth. She quickly devoured the rest of the éclair, and licked the last of the whipped cream that had made its way around her lips.

Jessica listened to the rhythm of the traffic as it passed by. The buzzing sound of the motorbikes, mixed with the horn beeps of cars and vans filled her ears with noise. Muffled beneath the sounds of the traffic was the call of the man at the market stall trying to sell bananas and strawberries. As she walked nearer towards him, she could smell the sweet aroma of the fruits filling her lungs, and the sound of him calling bellowed louder in her ears.

Jessica walked by, passing every shop and stall, not having the desire to look at anything being sold. Around her, all types of people moved about almost frantically, desparate to see someone or be somewhere: ladies armed with carrier bags of shopping dragging moaning children behind them, business men in suits and sunglasses talking on mobile phones, old ladies sat on benches chatting eating ice-creams. What a difference to the homeless people sat on blankets, looking sorrowful and forlorn with no hint of haste in them,having no place to go.

Ahead of her, Jessica spotted the surf shop, where her brother Darren worked. She decided to go inside and see him. Perhaps she was a little biased because her brother worked there, but it was one of the best shops on the high street Jessica thought, because it had the brightest and most colourful displays and the people who worked there actually loved surfing, so they were always friendly.

"Jessica!" her brother bellowed as soon as she took a step into the door. "What are you doing here?"
Jessica spotted her brother, leant on the counter with his girlfriend Laura stood next to him, chewing gum with huge bites in such a dramatic way, and fashioning a tight fitting skirt which hung just bellow her knicker line, accompanied by a tight fitting shirt that just about kept her breasts strapped inside it..Jessica's heart sank on seeing she was there.

"Are you ok?" he asked, looking a little worried on spotting her slightly dishevelled appearance. He decided not to say anything about the fact that Jessica normally took pride in the way she looked and moved away from the counter and over towards her.

"Yea, I'm ok," Jessica said, muffled in his arms as he wrapped them around her and gave her a big hug.

Jessica stayed there for a couple of seconds, but soon felt the tears beginning to well up, which she didn't want, so she pulled away.

Soon, Laura had made her way down the stairs and was standing at Darren's side.
"Hi Jess!" she said in a high pitched tone, beaming from ear to ear at Jessica, "Didn't fancy school then?" she asked. Jessica shook her head. "I don't blame you. School never did me any good!" she laughed. It was one of those annoying laughs that stood out from a crowd, and made people feel awkward on hearing it, almost like a hyena.

Darren must have read Jessica's mind, probably from the look of frustration that Jessica desperately tried to hide. "Hey Laura, Listen, I'm gonna take my break now and head out with Jess for a little bit. You ok here minding the shop with the other guys?"

Laura forced a smile, "Sure. Have fun!"

Fun? Jessica thought. was she out of her mind? How was it fun when her best friend had just died which meant the thought of going to school had filled her with dread. Little Miss Bimbo may have always taken the day off school because she couldn't be bothered, but this was totally different. What with her and the bus driver making his stupid comment earlier that day, Jessica felt she knew how it would feel to actually want to murder someone, and right now she had already lined up two of her victims.

"Hey, Jess, why don't we go and get a milkshake from somewhere?" Darren asked, interrupting her murderous thoughts of having Laura stabbed with a thick knife through her chest.

Turning to face her brother, to dispel the thoughts from her mind, Jessica replied, "I'd like that. Can we go to that new milkshake place in town?"
Darren looked at his watch. "Err. Yea, why not. I have about 20 minutes."

The two of them walked out of the shop and down towards the new American style diner that sold milkshakes of every variety with all the ingredients you could ever wish for. Jessica was already beginning to decide which flavour she was going to choose.

"So, what are your plans for the rest of the day?" her brother asked, looking down at her with a little look of concern.
"Well, I figured I would stay here for a while and then head back. I just wanted some time to clear my head. I'm a little worried about going back to school, I want to make sure I'm ok before I go, if you know what I mean." Jessica replied, trying to smile so as to let her brother know she was ok. She didn't want him to worry.
"You need to take all the time you need Jess. Don't rush, that way you'll be stronger in the long run." Her brother told her. He was so protective over Jessica. She loved it.

Before long, they were outside the dinner and looking at the milkshake menu.
"I think I'm going to have mint chocolate with extra cream and strawberries on top" Jessica beamed.
"You've chosen already?! What!" he jabbed her in the side with his elbow in a jokey way, "....ok....well I'll have the mango surprise, with extra cream and you can have whatever you like. I'll get them. I know why you came to see me now! Its not because you wanted to see your brother, its because you're after my money isn't it?!" Darren jabbed her in the side to tickle her. Jessica

jumped and let out one of her mouse like squeals. She always did that, and always felt a little embarrassed afterwards, wishing she could keep it inside, but it always just came out before she could stop. Darren laughed at her.

"Yep, you know me!" Jessica said, walking into the diner and heading over to some spare blue leather seats sat next to the window, whilst her brother went to make the order.

Jessica was glad she'd decided to see her brother. He always did cheer her up. She watched him ordering the milkshakes and before long he was walking over towards her.

"Hey Jess, listen, about earlier....with Laura. You know, she says things that she really doesn't mean sometimes. I don't think she realises it. You know that though, right?"

Jessica felt a little disheartened that Darren had reminded her. "Yes" Jessica sighed.

Darren realised this, and tried to change the subject by taking a big mouthful of milkshake, leaving a huge froth of cream all over his top lip which made Jessica laugh. He was such a goon sometimes, but that's why she loved him.

"You know, just so you don't take it personally Jess. I remember once, Laura made the most ridiculous comment to this old man who came into the shop. He was this little old man, really sweet and innocent. He wanted to buy some surfing shorts, because he'd booked his first surfing lesson. Everyone smiled and thought it was cool that he was going to try and surf. He must have been about 70. But Laura, she piped up with "Aren't you a little old for surfing? Shouldn't you be in to bowling?"

Some Souls Live Forever

Jessica stopped sucking the milkshake and stared at Darren open-mouthed. She shouldn't have been surprised because it was a typical Laura comment, but she was right

"I was so embarrassed" Darren continued, "But that's what I'm saying about Laura. She says out loud comments which probably other people think, but she actually says them." Darren smiled, looking over the top of his milkshake.

"Yea, lets not talk about Laura. I know she's your girlfriend, so I'll put up with her."

Jessica took a big mouthful of her milkshake, forcing it so much, it made a big slurping noise as she tried to suck the last remnants from the bottom of the glass. Normally she would never do this, but today she didn't care.

She noticed out of the corner of her eye, a rather large gentleman in the booth adjacent to where they sat, devouring donuts. He sat in a white sleeveless vest top with chest hair protruding from each of the edges. He was drooping over his plate like a dog protecting its find. He was so intent on devouring his plateful of donuts, and eating at such a speed that he had formed a sprinkling of sugar all around his mouth which he did not seem to care to remove. Clumps of sugar hung in his moustache, looking rather like big pieces of dandruff. The sight made Jessica feel sick, but she still felt sorry for the man. She was sure she had seen him in the café several times before. He looked lonesome. She wondered what life story he had, where he had been in the world and what he had done with his life.

As if the man had read Jessica's thoughts, he turned to look at Jessica, obviously noticing that she had been staring for a while. Jessica smiled at the man, with all her effort to make him feel happy. The man looked almost surprised, as though no one had smiled at him for years. He seemed to force a smile back at Jessica and then quickly returned to his task of finishing the plateful of donuts, stuffing another one into his mouth.

"Are you done?" Darren asked, causing her to look now at him.
"Err, yea, thanks Darren." She had realised she had once again got swept away with her thoughts.
"Time to go little one." Darren said, as he swung his legs out from the aisle and jumped to his feet.

Jessica hated him calling her 'little one.' It made her feel small and weak. She decided not to react to the comment as it was only because he cared, but at that moment she wanted to whack him, even if only playfully. She followed Darren out of the café into the sunshine. It made her eyes squint as soon as she stepped outside.

"Right little one, I've got to go. You walking back with me?" he asked, pulling on his sunglasses.

There it was again, that comment...little one. Jessica gritted her teeth and took a breath, "Err... no. I'm going to head back" Jessica said, looking down at the floor, kicking a discarded drinks can that lay on the floor by her feet. She didn't want to see Laura again, and there wasn't much else to do in town. Jessica felt like she wanted to be back at home.

"Ok, well you look after yourself, and if you need me, just call. Ok?" Darren asked. Jessica nodded her head. "Ok?" he asked again, not sure if Jessica had properly registered what he had said.
"Yea, ok!" she said, smiling this time, which made him smile back before he turned and walked off, almost bouncing down the road.

Some Souls Live Forever

The two of them parted ways, and Jessica turned to head towards the bus stop. She felt better for seeing Darren. Her thoughts wandered in daydreams, and before long she was at the bus stop. Just in time too, as the large yellow bus pulled in, its strong hot fumes forming in clouds in front of her. Trying not to breathe them in, she quickly got onto the bus where she took a lungful of air. The bus driver was a lady this time, with ginger curly hair fastened tightly behind her head, and mesmerising deep turquoise eyes that meant Jessica couldn't help but stare at them for a little while. The lady smiled at Jessica, as she flashed her return ticket, before walking towards her seat.

Jessica's thoughts switched to school. The thought of going back filled Jessica with fear. She was worried she wouldn't handle the pace and intensity of seeing lots of people again. It was challenging enough being in town, and she had only managed that for a little while. She thought that everyone would be asking about Blake too, so she would have to face the endless conversations of explaining what had happened. All throughout the journey home, these thoughts swam around in Jessica's head, causing her to worry. By the time she reached the bus stop outside her house, she felt deeply tired, like all she wanted to do was sleep.

Swiftly saying thank you to the driver and exiting the bus, Jessica made her way quickly into her house. Not stopping to take a look at the view, or to care much for anything, she walked straight into the house, and into her bedroom, where she flung herself onto her bed, nestling her head into her pillow. Within a few moments, she was asleep with thoughts of school still haunting her.

It wasn't until the front door banged that she awoke. It was her mum, coming into the house speaking on her mobile, with bags of groceries in her hands. Jessica leapt out of bed, realising she had been asleep for most of the afternoon, as the midday sun had dropped to a low place in the sky and there was now a coolness in the air.

Jessica heard her mum speaking to her grandma. Her voice sounded strained, as she was obviously struggling with the groceries. Jessica rubbed the sleepiness from her eyes and ruffled her hair, before crawling out of bed towards the living room. Waking up and moving so quickly gave her coloured spots in her eyes. Struggling to regain vision, she noticed her mum waving at her. Jessica waved back, and again rubbed her eyes.

Jessica's stomach rumbled, so deeply it felt like there was something moving in her belly she was so hungry. The silver clock on the wall showed it was 7 o'clock, which meant sleeping had caused her to skip lunch. She felt a little faint, so decided to flop down on the sofa. Her mum was still gassing away on the phone, discussing anything and everything it seemed.

Jessica decided to put the T.V. on. She flicked through the channels trying to find something of interest. She didn't really have much of a care to watch anything, almost in a daze, her brain giving up on absorbing anything new. Her mum had soon said her goodbyes on the phone and walked over to sit with Jessica.

"Hey sweetie. How you feeling?" she asked, pulling Jessica's hair from her eyes.
"Ok." Jessica said solemnly.
"I bought you some things. I got you some D.V.D.s and there's a sandwich for you in the fridge. I guessed you

missed lunch, because I popped in to see you and you were out for the count. Are you hungry now?"

Jessica nodded her head. Her mum then walked into the kitchen to fetch the sandwich. In a few seconds, she had returned, giving the plate to Jessica.

Jessica took the plate, feeling the icy cold on her hands. She suddenly felt an extreme hunger, that she couldn't get the sandwich to her lips quickly enough. Jessica hardly noticed that she was eating a cheese and pickle sandwich, she ate so quickly. Her mum put 'Romeo and Juliet' on and pulled the curtains closed to engulf her in darkness. She sat next to Jessica and put her arm around her.

Jessica finished eating her sandwich. She rested her head on her mum's shoulder and let herself forget her troubles and watch the film. Her and her mum stayed there, all evening, making all her troubles fade away, if only for a few hours.

Chapter 10

Waking up for her first day back at school was nerve-wracking to say the least. Normally, Blake and Jessica would walk together, chatting the whole way. Walking alone was strange. It meant Jessica's thoughts were left to herself, her mind free to wander. It kept tracking back to Blake and how much she missed him.

Just before she had left for school, Jessica had sat on the shoreline alone, with the sand nestled between her toes and the cool calm breeze upon her face. She had looked out to the ocean and made Blake a promise. It was to achieve everything they had always dreamed of doing. All the wishes and aims they had for the future, she was going to set out to achieve that year.

Blake being taken away from her had made Jessica realise how unpredictable life was, and how at any minute fate could twist and turn life 180 degrees. She was left in turmoil and sadness and longing for him to come back, but at the same time the realisation that she had to make the most of her life and grasp every opportunity. Life was happening now and she had a choice whether to embrace it, or to let what had happened change her life for the worst. Jessica thought about the situation if the roles had been reversed, and it had been her who was taken from Blake. She would want him to live his life fully for her, and she knew, deep in her heart that that was what he would want for her now.

On the walk to school, Jessica had mixed feelings. Her body almost ached and craved deeply for Blake to return, but she also had this new inner strength and desire to want to explore further what life had to offer which gave her energy.

Soon she arrived at the gates to Marylebone High School, where crowds of students were already flocking in before her. Laughter and loud voices could be heard everywhere as people were seen in reunion, catching up with each other's gossip, after the break. Jessica walked further into the gates. The nearest group of people were gathered, hunched over in a circle. This stopped when they detected her presence. Then, whispers echoed around the circle and soon everyone turned to face her. The atmosphere was tense, as a silence appeared and lasted far longer than felt comfortable. Jessica tried to force an awkward smile as she walked past, the group obviously not knowing what to say, their gaze following her, a few of them nodding their heads to acknowledge her, or breaking into weak smiles.

Another group of girls who were laughing and giggling in high pitched squeals also stopped the minute they saw Jessica. They tried hard to conceal the fact that they were watching her every time Jessica looked away, but Jessica knew eyes were on her. She was too cool to say any remark to them, but thought to herself she wished they had the emotional intelligence to simply say something, even if it was a simple "hello!". The staring gazes and silences caused an uneasiness in her stomach, that made her want to turn around and head straight back out of the gates.

Jessica was stronger than that. She continued past the group of girls, even summoning the energy to force a smile as she passed them, but she hastened her speed for the entrance to the school building, desperate to escape.

Strangely, amongst the awkwardness, a returning thought kept coming to Jessica's mind – something that she had heard before, but where from, she could not remember. She kept remembering something that someone had told her once – "that sometimes in the moment of crisis in our lives that we find out who we truly are, that we get to learn more about ourselves, and meet a new person inside us". It did make sense to her right now, as entering the school building without Blake by her side, she was having to be brave and find a new, stronger person to take on the year without her soul mate.

As soon as Jessica pulled open the large oak door with the small rectangular frosted window pane, she was met with an enthusiastic cry, "Jessica! Jessica!" a call from along the hallway. It was her form tutor Miss Button. Jessica turned to face her tutor, who was bounding up the hallway towards her, dressed in a floral skirt and flip flops, glasses perched on top of her head from which pieces of hair were flying everywhere, appearing as if she had just gotten out of bed.

Miss Button looked in a flap, as always, clutching several folders and walking quickly. Jessica thought very fondly of Miss Button, she always was one of her favourite tutors because she was so funny, and down-to-earth. She was someone who you could have a laugh with, not just an institutional robot, like some of the other tutors. She possessed a true kindness, and an ability to win over her students, by the care and attention that she showed each of them, always checking that they were happy and settled and going that extra mile to make sure that was the case.

"I'm so glad I've caught you Jessica!" Miss Button exclaimed, "You were one of my top priorities today, I just.....well..." nearly dropping one of her folders which almost slipped from her grip, Miss Button continued, "I just wanted to say to you how I know this year is going to be tough, but we are all here behind you, supporting every step of the way. I know Blake was a very special person and we need to do something in school to remember him, but we can think about that and talk it through together to choose something you would really like...."

Jessica could feel her eyes beginning to well up again. Talking about remembering Blake was another of those moments where a shotgun blasted into her chest at the realisation that this was not a dream and that it really had happened.

"Jessica? What do you think lovely?...." Jessica realised she had missed much of the end of the conversation, getting lost away somewhere with her thoughts, in a distant place. It was as though the words were coming too fast for her to digest them. She felt embarrassed.
"I'm sorry, I....err....I think the memorial is great, it's just, I don't feel so great, I think I need to sit down, I feel really sick...." Jessica had spotted the chairs by reception during the conversation and now swiftly worked her way over to them, where she flopped down. Miss Button followed and watched Jessica put her head into her hands, overcome with feelings of nausea. Bending down in front of her, so that Jessica could see her, Miss Button took one of her hands very gently and held it with both of hers. Jessica looked up into her eyes.

"No-one can tell you how you should be feeling right now. No-one can imagine how difficult this is. It would help if you could tell us what is going to make things better for you, but there is no rush. You have to do everything in your own time." Miss Button smiled.

Fighting back the tears, Jessica cleared her throat, "I'm ok. It's Strange…" Miss Button knew Blake very well, so Jessica knew she would understand when she told her she was about to, "I feel like Blake is still here. I don't think he is dead and that's it, he's gone. I think his spirit is still here. Not as a ghost either, not that kind of spirit. More that he is around everywhere, and I keep getting these thoughts that my life is going to change, that I am going to change."

Jessica looked at Miss Button, who looked interested, hanging onto every word that Jessica spoke, "I feel as though he is guiding me somehow…." Jessica hesitated for a second,

"What is he telling you, Jessica?" Miss Button asked. Her soft, gentle voice was comforting, reassuring.

Jessica looked into Miss Button's eyes, deeply this time. She wanted to see if Miss Button was truly believing her, and not thinking she was strange. When she looked, she got the feeling of comfort that she needed, "He is telling me that I will find a new strength to live a better life…..its strange I know."

Jessica thought she could see tears begin to well up in Miss Button's eyes. She said nothing, but had an encouraging look that gestured for Jessica to continue. "I really believe Blake wants me to go out and do everything we said we would do together, and more. He wants me to kind of…."

"Live life fully and make every day matter?" Miss Button finished the sentence.

"Yeah." At that minute, Jessica felt a surge of relief that she had managed to tell someone how she truly felt.

Since the funeral, she had kept feeling this way, but not telling anyone else about it because she felt guilty for feeling positive. Jessica thought that everyone would expect her to be locked away in her bedroom, crying all day, longing for Blake. She felt some pangs of guilt that she wasn't doing that so soon after hearing the news, but instead had some hope for the future. It was true that she had felt totally deflated since hearing the news, but this new positivity was becoming stronger every moment.

Miss Button squeezed Jessica's hand, "You are a strong person Jessica. We both know Blake well and know exactly what he would say to you. I think your positivity is brilliant. Keep believing that, and keep holding on to your inner strength. On those days where you feel you may not have that strength, I'm always here for you Jessica, so come and find me if you ever need to talk. It doesn't have to be about sadness either - if you want to just chat, come find me." Miss Button gave Jessica's hand one last squeeze, before standing up. Jessica smiled at her.

As Miss Button walked off, her floral skirt swaying from side to side with each stride, Jessica's thoughts drifted back to the conversation. She wondered why Miss Button had understood so well. Perhaps she had too lost a close friend.
The bell rang, and the once silent reception and hallway became a mass of students travelling in all directions. Noise and commotion filled every inch of space that was, moments ago completely vacant.

Chapter 11

Jessica's first lesson was Maths. She had tried hard to concentrate, but mainly had found herself gazing out of the window, watching the clouds drift slowly across the sky, painting a new picture every few moments.

Every so often, Jessica would realise her trance like state, and suddenly snap back into reality. Then she would hastily try to complete several of the multiplication sums that Mr Rawton had set for the class in an attempt to catch up, but this would only ever last for a few minutes, before she would find herself staring once again out at the cotton wool like clouds as they set new scenes for her to appreciate.

She was sure that Mr Rawton had noticed that she had hardly completed any work in the lesson, but he seemed to just leave her alone.

Soon, the piercing bell sounded again, and it was time for the next lesson, English. Jessica fondly loved English lessons, particularly creative writing. Her free spirit loved to explore her vivid imagination and let her thoughts run free to create distant lands or places where she could escape to, like tropical beaches with glorious sands, or mysterious forests where a knight in shining armour would come to save the day. She hoped desperately that today would be a day where she would be allowed the opportunity to express herself in this way, as she had a lot she wanted to say.

Jessica had spent most of the morning so far by herself, as although in a crowd, it was spent in solitude, with her thoughts by herself. As she entered the classroom, Mrs Upton sat, cross legged on top of her desk. This was a good sign, Jessica thought, as Mrs Upton looked relaxed and at ease, so creative writing could be on the cards. It certainly wasn't going to be a factual lesson.

Mrs Upton was a funny lady, but someone who everyone enjoyed having as their teacher. She had bright auburn hair, always straightened so that it lay flatly against her pale skin. Her green eyes, looked similar to that of a cat, with an air of mysteriousness that seemed as though they spoke to anyone who looked at them, as if saying there were lots of secrets about Mrs Upton that everyone would like to know. Mrs Upton was a lady with a real passion for English. Whenever she spoke, it was using dramatic tones that carried in the air, filling the room.

Jessica positioned herself towards the back of the class, discarding her bag down by the side of the table and pulling the chair out to sit down. She knew Mrs Upton was watching her intently, but she didn't want to look up and make eye contact, because Jessica was worried that this may cause her to let out a tear. Mrs Upton was one of those teachers who always delved deeper than others, and got to know her students on a personal level.

Jessica gazed around the room, looking at everyone and seeing if she could spot changes from the summer. Several people now sported a tan, or had new haircuts. As her eyes wandered around the room, two of her friends, Beth and Hannah turned around simultaneously and faced her. Both smiled at her and waved. Jessica returned their gestures. Finally! Two friends who didn't think that she had caught some dreaded lurgy, who were willing to acknowledge her. As Mrs Upton began speaking, the two girls rotated back to face the front of the classroom.

"Well, some of you are going to absolutely love this lesson, and others of you are not. I want to find out all about your summer holidays, and what better a way to do this than a creative writing lesson!"

Jessica instantly felt enthused at the prospect. This is what she needed. A chance to let words flow freely, and let out her emotions. As Mrs Upton had continued talking, she had informed the class that it was a session of free choice, be it poetry, or stories or drama, they could choose how they wanted to show her what had happened in their summer holidays.

Mrs Upton was now positioned adjacent to Jessica's individual table and bent over in an attempt to make eye contact with her.

"Jessica!" Mrs Upton called, then lowered her voice to a softer, more delicate tone, "How do you feel about this task? You see, we know what happened this summer and if this is totally not what you need, then please tell me and I can excuse you to go and do something else in the ICT suite or something."

"Actually, Mrs Upton..." Jessica looked up at the red rectangular spectacles perched on the end of Mrs Upton's rather long nose, that now looked down at her. "I would love to do some creative writing." Jessica responded timidly, a little overwhelmed by Mrs Upton, "I think this is what I need to do," she said, looking down at top sheet of the two blank pieces of paper that had been put on her desk by one of the helpers, and began doodling a flower in the corner.

"Fantastic, well you know me lovely!" Mrs Upton exclaimed, "Get your creative juices flowing – the more creativity the better!" Mrs Upton stood up in a flash and walked off towards a dark haired pupil who had his hand poised in the air, ready for some attention.

Some Souls Live Forever

'Right!' thought Jessica, 'It's my space and my time to write what I want!" She let her mind wander a little more, and then picked up her sparkly blue pencil. Twiddling it between her thumb and finger for a while, Jessica then decided on a poem. She was going to write a poem to Blake.

Putting her pen a little cautiously to paper, Jessica began writing, "Dear Blake," she stopped, pondered for a while and then crossed out the words and started again "Blake. You were my hero." Jessica stopped again, this time with a hint of frustration. She screwed up the paper into a tight ball, and put it firmly on the corner of her table.

Taking a deep breath, Jessica realised she shouldn't force the situation. The words needed to flow. What was it that she really wanted to say to Blake? Suddenly, it came to her, the first two lines,

"You were my light in life that brightened every day,
Bringing sunshine into my life in every way."

Re-reading the rhyming couplet made her realise she was now on track. Thinking for a moment, Jessica then continued,
"Your light burned with a magical flame that danced everywhere you went,
Giving everyone a glowing feeling inside with the warmth that it sent."

Jessica realised she was now on to something, she had that feeling that the poem sounded right. This happened with her. Sometimes, meaningful words that rhymed just came easily to her mind.
"Your smile made me smile, even if I was sad and didn't want to.

Your eyes made me feel alive, no matter if I was tired, you made me feel brand new,"

Jessica found herself totally absorbed for the remainder of the English lesson. She felt totally engaged with the work. Not like maths, with its rigid frameworks and right and wrong answers. Jessica didn't much care for formality. By the time Mrs Upton had signalled it was time to stop working and for children to share work, Jessica had finished her poem and re-read it several times.

Mrs Upton smiled sweetly, as she asked the class,
"Who would like to read or show their magical piece of creativity to the class?"
Jessica felt compelled. She wanted to share her work, so put her hand up rigidly, sure that she would be picked.
Mrs Upton scanned the room looking for the right candidate for the job. Almost perplexed at the sight of Jessica putting up her hand, Mrs Upton responded.
"Jessica, would you like to come to the front and share your work?"

At that very moment, almost every head in the room turned around to gawp at Jessica, who felt a surge of nervousness at the reaction.
"Hmmm....ok." she said, swallowing the saliva that had gathered in her throat.

Jessica picking up her paper, feeling sweat on her hands. She remembered the last time she had felt this, it had been at the funeral. Quickly, she cleared her throat and diverted her thoughts to the task.

As she pushed her chair backwards to stand up, it sent a screeching sound into the classroom, as the chair legs pushed across the tiled floor. Jessica could feel the hairs twitching on the inside of her ears. Ignoring this, she quickly walked to the front of the room, and stood next to Mrs Upton, who had returned to her cross-legged position on the table. Not many teachers were as relaxed as Mrs Upton, but that is half of the reason why most people really liked her – she didn't even try to appear too formal, she wanted her students to feel welcome and on a par with her.

As Jessica looked down at the paper, her blond ringlets fell into her vision. She carefully pulled them behind her ears, and looked up at the faces looking back at her. Some were smiling encouragingly. Others looked almost on the edge of their seats with anticipation with what Jessica was to reveal.

Taking a sigh, Jessica began,
"You were my light in life that brightened every day,
Bringing sunshine into my life in every way.
 Your light burned with a magical flame that danced everywhere you went,
Giving everyone a glowing feeling inside with the warmth that it sent.

Your smile made me smile, even if I was sad and didn't want to.
Your eyes made me feel alive, no matter if I was tired, you made me feel brand new!
Embraced in your arms is where I felt I belonged,
Lying on the beach, singing our favourite song.

Now you're gone, it seems life is like a huge mountain that I have to climb,
I'm taking huge steps every day, getting nearer to the summit each time,

But I've realised that my life is not just about the climbing,
The richness of life truly comes in the finding,

That life is about embracing those moments when you stop and look at the view,
Seeing the beauty of life, the trees so luscious green and the sky so dazzling blue,
Watching the sparkles on the sea dancing so gracefully,
Seeing the birds soaring high, spreading their wings and gliding elegantly,

Even though it seems you're gone Blake, and I feel scared without you,
I'm going to remember to stop and think that you're there in that view,
You are there in those trees, that sky, with the birds, in the sea,
No matter where I go, you'll always be with me.

I know that because we made a vow to each other,
That we would be friends together forever,
Our circles of our souls are joined and can't be broken,
That was our very special token.

Of your love for me, and my love for you,
And that Blake, will always be true.

I know your soul is in a higher place watching me and protecting me,
Even though sometimes it feels your gone and have been set free.
My circle is still here, linked with yours, in that higher place,
Until that special day when one day our souls will meet again, face to face.

Some Souls Live Forever

I know you loved me, and you know I'll always love you,
That Blake, is a precious promise we made that will
always be true.

The room was sat in absolute motionless silence. Not
even the catch of a breath could be heard in the room.

Even Mrs Upton could not summon a response for
several moments, until, with a flustered reaction, she
said,
"Jessica, that was beautiful. Such vivid imagery created,
and contemplative stanzas. I think.." she said, looking at
the class, "we deserve to acknowledge the effort put into
this!" Everyone in the room began clapping. It was a
reaction that Jessica knew lasted longer than was
usually the case when someone had shared a good
piece of work which made her feel warm inside

The atmosphere in the room had changed, as though
every person in that room wanted to reach out and
touch Jessica and hold her close. She really felt as
though she had connected with the hearts of every
person in that room. As she looked up from her paper
and towards the class, she was met with an array of
smiles. Even Justin, the most arrogant self righteous
idiot in the class raised his eye brows which meant he
enjoyed listening to her poem. Not that Jessica would
have cared much if he didn't, because this was about
Blake and her, finally all her classmates would have to
face the fact that this had happened and she needed
them to act normally around her, not pretend that
nothing had happened. That would not be fair to Blake
or to her, as his memory needed to live on, forever.

Chapter 12

Lunchtime followed English. It couldn't come soon enough, as Jessica felt the pangs of hunger deep in her belly. As she gathered her belongings together, and handed in her poem to Mrs Upton, Jessica found herself being escorted by two friends on either side of her. One was Hannah, and the other Beth. Each of them were talking to her at such a quick pace, she almost felt dizzy.

"So, Beth and I were thinking we could go and catch a movie sometime soon. They've got loads of cool stuff on...." Hannah bellowed across Jessica's path towards Beth.
"Yeah totally cool films showing at the mo, and that new cinema down by Ocean Seven looks really cool." Beth returned, "What do you think Jess?" Beth asked.

"Yeah ok, sounds great" Jessica returned, looking at Beth who sported a hair style, now straightened flat against her head, with tints of dye intermingled with the brown.
She was a really pretty girl, with freckles dotted all over her face, which had a softness to it that gave a comforting feeling. She was popular with everyone, but thankfully popular for the right reasons, because she was a nice person.

Hannah was the same, with a heart of gold for everyone around her. Her shiny blond was always beautifully plaited neatly and fastened with grips to her hair. Never could a stray hair be seen, for the attention given to it was the same as the attention she gave to everyone she knew.

Some Souls Live Forever

Jessica wished she knew Hannah and Beth more than she did, as although she often worked with them in lessons, usually by choice, it was Blake who she spent her spare time in school with. Hannah and Beth were friends with Jessica because they shared the same English and French classes, and so any time they needed to do group work, the three of them would naturally gravitate towards each other. Both of them were friendly enough, and happy, but Jessica had never really felt a real connection with them. They were more town girls than Jessica. They would spend their time in town or shopping, not like Jessica who much preferred the calm atmosphere of the sea where she could chill out. Still, at least they were genuine people who were making the effort. Jessica felt instantly better that people were involving her.

The three girls moved out towards the hallway and headed for the canteen, following the aroma of the chips that lured their senses. The two girls continued chatting to Jessica as they walked towards the canteen, talking endlessly about their holidays, gossip circulating around the school and about what movies they wanted to watch. Jessica dipped in and out of the conversation, but was intrigued more about the prospect of lunch. Managing to jostle with the crowds and somehow find a place in the queue, the three of them awaited eagerly for their chips.

Children of all appearances filtered in and out of the canteen in all directions. Jessica found her way through the gaps, with the odd elbow being shoved her way as people fought to get to the front of the queue. If Blake had been here, Jessica thought, he would have protected her, and people would have not even considered barging in front of him, because his tall athletic body gave a presence that he was one not to be fooled with.

Hannah and Beth were chatting away on either side of Jessica. Normally she was the bubbly one, always having a lot to say, but not today. It was all still a bit of a shock, and not having Blake by her side at all the usual places they would meet in the school day, made her keep remembering what had happened. Not that she ever forgot what had happened anyway, but it made it even more real. It made her realise that she was always with Blake wherever he went, almost as though she was his shadow following him around. He was the talented sportsman, the artist, the mathematician, popular with everyone. Jessica was popular too, but many of her friends were her friends because they liked Blake, especially the boys who wanted to be like him.

Soon, Jessica was called by the dinner lady, dressed in a pink chequered jacket with a white cap on her head, "Wakey wakey sunshine!" she called out, revealing the gap at the front of her teeth which made Jessica think she could look remarkably like a pirate if she wore a pirate hat. Jessica snapped back into reality, seeing she had made her way to the front of the dinner queue, now being offered her bowl of chips and cheese. Turning around to find a space, Jessica scanned the room. Finding a place to eat was going to be an arduous task as row upon row of students lined the canteen seats, munching away. As Beth and Ellie joined her, they walked over to the far corner where an unseated bench could be seen. There they sat themselves eager to taste the chips on their lips.
Soon conversation stopped, and the three of them sat munching, tunnelling away without looking up until at least half their bowl of chips had disappeared.

Some Souls Live Forever

Jessica wanted to make conversation, but for the first time in her life, she realised what it was like to be a nervous person. Normally at the forefront of conversation, today she sat, feeling an urge to speak, but somehow not actually managing to form any words. Beth and Hannah must have realised this, because they kept looking up from their plates towards Jessica, as if to encourage her to talk to them.

Feeling very uncomfortable, Jessica quickly finished her chips, hardly tasting them, and decided to make excuses to leave the table. She wasn't in the correct frame of mind to make small talk, even if she wanted to.

"Right guys, I'm going to head off because I said I would catch up with the headmaster Mr Snithe to talk to him about Blake." Jessica stood up, and pitched a false smile at both of her friends.

"Ok, see you later Jess!" Beth said joyfully. Hannah was still chewing on the food in her mouth, but waved at Jessica and tried to smile, despite the bulging food which made her look a little like a hamster.

Jessica swiftly dismissed herself and walked through the rows of benches towards the door. She felt a sense of relief that she was no longer around Beth and Hannah. It wasn't that she didn't like them, on the contrary they were really lovely people, but she just felt an urge to be by herself.

Jessica hadn't actually planned on going to see Mr Snithe, that was just her excuse for leaving, but now she was out of the canteen, she had to decide where to go.

All of a sudden, Miss Button was in sight, approaching her. Looking as if she were on a mission again, but working her way, it seemed, towards Jessica.

"Jessica?" Miss Button called out rather urgently, "Jessica?" she called again.

"Yes?" Jessica returned, in slight nervous anticipation as to why she was being called.

"Just wondering if you could follow me down to my office? You're not in trouble at all, in fact there is something very exciting to share with you." Miss Button was beaming another of those infectious smiles that made Jessica instantly light up, despite how she was feeling deep inside.

She followed Miss Button down the corridor towards the blue door of her office, which opened up to a small rectangular room stacked high with shelf upon shelf of text books. On the small oak table lay a computer and small lamp, and several framed photos of young children. As soon as Jessica was in the office, Miss Button swiftly shut the door behind her and turned to face Jessica with that beaming smile. She was clutching a pile of papers in her arms. Jessica was intrigued. She picked up on the atmosphere that there was some good news, though she couldn't at all think what this could be.

"Jessica, I want to make you an offer. You don't have to take me up on this – though I think you should!" Miss Button looked down at the papers which she had lowered from her chest to acknowledge that the answer to her enthusiasm lie in them. She quickly looked back at Jessica, "I meant to tell you this earlier before school finished last year, that I submitted the work that you did for your end of year project which you dedicated to raising awareness of conservation projects around the world, to the World Animal Trust, because I was so impressed by the care and effort you put into it, that I thought it deserved recognition.

Some Souls Live Forever

Jessica thought back to the hours she had put into her geography project the previous summer before term had ended. Jessica was passionate about animals and the environment. She was so enthused by the topic of raising awareness of conservation projects last year, that she had in addition to all her research and project work, organised all sorts of music and arts events for the whole school to raise money for the World Animal Trust, and she had even managed to encourage many students and parents to write campaign letters to members of government and local newspapers in an attempt to really make a difference.

Miss Button continued, interrupting her thoughts, "Well, I received this morning a letter from the World Animal Trust who are working at the moment out in Sri Lanka, they are responsible for a conservation project running out there looking after orphan orang-utans." Miss Button continued to smile as she spoke, and with a burst of energy, she exclaimed, "You're not going to believe this Jessica!. They were so impressed that they have offered you the opportunity to go out to Sri Lanka for 10 days at the animal sanctuary and help look after the chimpanzees in the orphanage along with a teacher! The letter says it all! It seems, they are offering one pupil place and one teacher place to lots of schools all over the country realising that school involvement really can make a difference, so now many other selected schools with enthusiasts like you will get the chance to all meet up and fly out together as part of a new national youth project promoting world conservation. It's a fantastic once in a lifetime opportunity, not to be missed!"

Jessica felt for the first time in a long while, uncontrollable happiness. Pure bursts of energy running throughout her veins, like mini fireworks being set off all over her body.

Jessica elatedly blurted out, "What, really?" with a look of complete elation. Miss Button nodded her head enthusiastically. Jessica couldn't really believe her ears. It was all too much to take in. "What, so you mean, you and I have been invited out to Sri Lanka for a whole 10 days? That sounds amazing, and I'd definitely like to go, but I don't really understand. If the Trust needs money, why would they offer such a trip for free?" Jessica asked.

"Well, that is because we would have to raise some money for the orphanage through the school like you did last year, and we would have to promise to promote what good work they are doing for years to come. There would also be newspaper articles which you would have to be involved in and possibly some T.V. coverage in youth News programmes. This would promote the orphanage and give people the chance to offer sponsorship, so actually they would make a lot of money."

Jessica began to feel more and more excited with each second. She felt herself smiling gleefully at Miss Button, who returned the gesture.
"So when do we go then?" she asked inquisitively.
"You won't believe this either," Miss Button exclaimed, "Its next week!"
Jessica surprised herself as she began laughing, this had been the most crazy week of her life. First the news of losing her best friend, and now this. She felt as though she was a puppet on a string, being pulled in all sorts of directions, all the strings attached to her heart. It made her begin to feel emotional again.

Some Souls Live Forever

Jessica began crying and looked down at the floor. Miss Button put the sheets of paper down on her desk and put a gentle hand on Jessica's shoulder. She tried to soothe Jessica, by telling her it was ok, and rubbing her shoulder.

Between sniffs, Jessica managed to communicate what was happening.

"It's just....well it's not really fair is it? Blake will never ever get to do anything like this again, and well I don't really feel I deserve it."

Miss Button instantly stopped Jessica and held her by her shoulders with both hands,

"Jessica, look at me." Jessica wiped her tears with her fingers, and looked at Miss Button, "You are a really special girl. I'm going to tell you something now. Something that Mr Snithe said, and I expect it will surprise you. Now he can be a bit of a meanie sometimes, but really he has a soft side. He's like.....how can I describe him?" Miss Button thought for a while, then continued, "He's like a crème egg, hard on the outside, but with a soft chewy middle."

Jessica laughed, wiping her nose with her sleeve. Mr Snithe was the head teacher, and speaking about him in this way to a teacher seemed rather bizarre.

"Well anyway, when I asked Mr Snit he about whether I could take you on this trip, he told me you would be the perfect candidate. He told me that you are a special person because you always encourage everyone around you, and you have a calming persona that makes all your friends happy and content. On top of this, anything you do, like this conservation awareness work you did last year, you never took credit for, it was completely unselfish and only motivated by your desire to want to help make the world a better place. You,

Jessica, care more for other people than you do yourself, and that is the greatest gift anyone can have."
Miss Button had sat herself on the desk as she said this, and continued to look at Jessica, who had now managed to stop crying and calm herself.

Now, she didn't know what to say. "I know how you are feeling Jessica, it's been a very taxing few days. Why don't you take this letter home to your parents and have a talk with them, and then let me know for definite tomorrow." Miss Button said, with an encouraging look.

Jessica nodded her head, and took the letter. She thought again about if the roles had been reversed, and what she would want Blake to do if it were him in this situation. Of course she would want him to go.
" I do really want to go! It would be great, and I love orang-utans!" Jessica took the letter to show her parents.

Mrs Button sighed with relief and jumped off the table to open the door for Jessica,
"See you tomorrow Jessica!" Miss Button called with a hint of animation.
"See you tomorrow!" Jessica returned. Walking out of the office was a new Jessica, different to the one that entered, because now all the feelings of hope that she had tried to summon herself over the last few days were being reciprocated, and now she really did have something to feel positive about, and to look forward to.

Chapter 13

The rest of the afternoon had passed quickly. It had been a double session of art, making clay sculptures. Jessica had been aware of everything occurring around her, boys being silly and throwing pieces of clay at each other, and various shapes emerging all around, but she mostly had been focused on her own work, and keeping her thoughts to herself introspectively. She had decided on making a seahorse, using her creative flair with excellence to mould and shape the clay into a stunning masterpiece.

Jessica had liked the feel of the soft cool clay on her hands. She enjoyed contouring the mixture, and feeling it ooze between the gaps in her hands as the squeezed it in clenched fists. It sent her daydreaming, slipping away into calmness every time she squished and squashed the clay with her hands.

Jessica had delicately smoothed the soft clay into a seahorse's body. Being careful so that every inch of the grey mixture was smooth without a single crease or notch, Jessica finally accepted it as being good enough and began to apply the features. With thoughtful consideration for an intricate pattern, Jessica had used her clay fork to etch swirls into the body, in the style of waves in the sea and attached several spikes and a tail to its body. As the seahorse emerged from its once shapeless lump, more and more pupils around her had noticed and pointed to share their admiration.

Mostly, Jessica had ignored them. Again, unlike her, as normally she would revel in the attention, today she focused her thoughts on the conservation project. She remembered reading about Sri Lanka once before whilst browsing the internet for some geography homework. She remembered the exotic greenery about in the rainforests, and the exuberant colours of the different flowers which came in all shapes and sizes. Jessica knew a handful of facts about the orang-utans – that they were native to Sri Lanka, the orange haired furry creatures living in family groups. She remembered watching a video of them swinging high from tree to tree, their long arms outstretched as they swung swiftly through the trees.

Jessica couldn't actually believe that she could have the chance to venture out there and feel the warmth of their bodies on hers when she imagined tending them and giving the baby orphans their milk. All sorts of questions came into her mind, like where they would be staying and how hot the temperature would be. All of this was so very exciting to Jessica. She really felt that the emotional rollercoaster she had been riding was finally on the up.

It was so lovely too, for her to recall the compliments that Miss Button had paid to her, because she didn't really realise what the teachers all thought of her, it hadn't really entered her mind before. Jessica felt uplifted from the praise and for the excitement of her adventure ahead.

Thankfully the end of the lesson came soon, because Jessica had a burning urge to get herself home as quickly as she could, so that she could share the news with her parents. As soon as the bell rang, signalling home time, and all the class were dismissed, Jessica quickly said her goodbyes to her fellow classmates and abruptly ran out of the school gates towards home, not of course, forgetting the letter that Miss Button had given her.

Some Souls Live Forever

Feeling completely exhausted by the run home in the blistering heat of a scorching hot day, and struggling to catch a breath, Jessica finally reached her home. As soon as she got there, she bounded up the stairs, not getting to her front door quickly enough. As soon as her hand touched the white door, she swung it open with such a force that it crashed against the chair inside the living room, and catapulted back, nearly catching her in the face, if she hadn't have had her hand there to prevent it.

Inside, Jessica was met with both her parents, in conversation it seemed, her father's back facing her, talking to her mother sat on the sofa.
"I have some great news!" Jessica called out to her parents, "You won't believe it!" she said, reiterating Miss Button's words.

Both her parents listened with intrigue, eager that their daughter seem so vibrant and full of energy. Jessica began talking quickly, hardly pausing to draw breath,
"Well, Miss Button gave me this letter, and she told me that she wants me to go with her on a special trip abroad – to Sri Lanka – where I can go and help look after the Orang-utans in their orphanage, helping to rear the young. Isn't it great?! It's for ten days."

Jessica thrust the letter forward to her father, who quickly took it in haste and began scanning the writing. All three sat quietly watching for his reaction at the letter.
"This looks fabulous Jessica, you should definitely go! What a brilliant....oh."
her dad abruptly stopped in his tracks, and began scratching his head with his hands.

"What?" Jessica's mum asked, now standing up beside her father.

"Well, look at the dates Anna....it's next week!" he handed the paper over and now began stroking his beard with one hand as if deep in thought, his other hand on his hip, signalling a hint of anger.

"I know it's short notice" Jessica said, "but that's ok isn't it? Why should the date be a problem?" Jessica asked.

"Well" her mum began, " Jessica, your dad has had some good news too. This morning he received a phone call from Italy, from the exhibition hall we went to in Rome. Do you remember that one?" Jessica nodded her head, of course she did, the thoughts of Italy returning now to the forefront of her mind.
"Well, one of the top agents there in Rome would like to set up a permanent exhibition, which will be open to the public. That means your dad will receive a large payment in advance, and from then on regular commission, and the earnings are going to start shooting through the roof, if it turns out to be a success, which of course it will!" her mum exclaimed, pitching a huge grin at her husband.

Jessica struggled to understand the link, as to why this was an issue for her. She hesitated. Her dad realised all was not fully explained, "Well Jessie, it means I have to fly out to Rome next week, because they want to run a photo shoot so that they can display my portrait in the exhibition."
"Oh!" Jessica said, disappointed, feeling like a lead balloon was dropped in her stomach as she realised. Jessica had been away with her father on every exhibition that displayed his work that he had ever been to. The whole family would go, as a way of showing their

belief in him that he really was going to fulfil his life-long dream. She couldn't possibly let him down, especially now that it seemed there was a chance everything could be set in motion for him to become the artist he had always aspired to.

"Ok! Jessica said, "Well, it doesn't matter, I'm sure there are plenty of other trips I can go on, or maybe they can change the dates that we go."
For a few moments, no one responded to Jessica, both of her parents stood motionless pondering for a while about the confusing situation. Jessica found her mum looking at her with an inquisitive look on her face, as if in thought as to how she could rectify the problem.

"Well, I think, even despite the fact that you want to support me, you should go on the conservation project Jessica!" he dad piped up quickly, "I think you should go anyway. I have the best family in the world, and you have always supported me my whole life, coming with me on every trip that I have been to. This is your chance Jessica to do something special for yourself."

"No" Jessica tried to resist, wanting to revel in her dad's success with him, "It's ok honestly, I want to be there to see the exhibition and to celebrate with you" she said, with a tone of disappointment that she tried to mask with some enthusiasm.
.

"Actually Jessica, I think you should listen to your father" her mother said, with a hint of a teacher voice, like she was in the classroom "You have been the greatest daughter we could have ever wished for, and do you know something Jessica. There is something very special about you, which both of us noticed since you were first born. You are one of the least selfish people we know. You always put others before yourself, and your real strengths in life rely on your compassion for others and your nature to think about everyone."

This was odd. Really odd. Jessica recalled Miss Button saying similar things to her earlier and now her mother sending the same message on the same day, without any reason for the connection. It wasn't as though this happened all the time, and she received such compliments regularly. No, in fact it was rare. Jessica wondered if it was Blake having an influence and trying to tell her something through the people that she knew. Before she could think about this much further, her dad intervened,

"Jessie, your mum is right. I would be devastated for you if you didn't grab hold of this opportunity with both hands. It's your chance to live an experience which probably won't come again. Go for it!" he said, casting a genuine look her way.

Jessica felt a little confused now. The pinnacle of enthusiasm that she felt earlier had now been curbed, and she was now left somewhere half way between ecstatic at the once in a lifetime opportunity, and upset that she couldn't support her dad like she would want to. She tried to force a smile, and made her way to the sofa to sit down. She watched her mum and dad read intently the letter both leaning over the paper together and absorbing all the details.

"You should feel very proud that you were chosen Jessica, because there is only pupil that has been invited." her mum said, "That shows how special you are doesn't it?!"

Jessica smiled again at her mum, thinking again she sounded like a teacher in a classroom. She began fiddling with the tassels on the carpet with her toes, waiting for them to finish reading the letter. Soon her mother joined her on the sofa. Her dad stood over them, "Jessica. You deserve this." He said. Jessica could tell he really meant it, with one hundred percent certainty, but he was obviously a little disappointed. Jessica didn't know what else to say. He walked off into the kitchen.

Jessica's mum put out her arm, signalling for Jessica to snuggle up to her for a hug. She leant over and rested her head onto her mother's shoulder, who began stroking her hair. Jessica began to feel more and more relaxed, as she felt the comfort of her mum's nails gently scratching her head, and running through the strands of her hair. She could feel the rhythmic pulse of her mum's heartbeat under her head, which was rested on her chest.

Chapter 14

It was dark when Jessica awoke feeling the chill of the evening air causing her to stir. She must have fallen asleep on the sofa yet again, despite having slept a great deal over the past few days. The light of the moonlight shone in through the curtains in streams of pure white light. Rapidly blinking in an attempt to regain her vision, Jessica realised she was alone in the room. The wind had obviously picked up outside, as she could hear the shutters on the windows repeatedly crashing against the walls and the muffled sounds of the waves slapping against the shoreline.

Jessica didn't much like the atmosphere. There was a strange feeling in the air. She walked over to the window which faced out towards the sea, and stood for a while gazing out to the sea. The moon shone like a pure white torch hung low in the sky. Shining stars scattered across the sky, giving a magical glow. A mystical blue line separated the sky from the sea, where waves rippled in lines stretching from the shore to the horizon. Jessica focused her eyes on the spots of white that shone like diamonds as each of the waves ripples moved across the sea.

Following the line of the shore, Jessica looked up to where she saw two silhouetted figures walking along the beach arm in arm. The figure of the man held the lady around her shoulder tightly, and both of them walked with the same footsteps, nearly in synchronised motion. The figures stopped for a while, as the man pointed up to the sky above them. Jessica tried to imagine what the conversation would be. She decided the man would be naming the star after the lady as a romantic gesture. Soon the figures began walking again, and before long they were nearly horizontal with Jessica's home. She could hear the lady laughing with a cackling sound at the man who seemed by the muffled tone of his gruff voice to be cracking jokes in an attempt it seemed, to impress her.

Jessica moved her eye line from the couple and back out the sea again. Now she thought about Blake again, and imagined her and him walking along the beach together arm and arm, just as the couple had done. They weren't boyfriend and girlfriend, but Blake was her close friend and soul mate, so they would have been sure to have walked just as the couple had done in time.

Jessica missed Blake so much. She longed to see him. It seemed like a whole lifetime since she had last looked into his deep blue eyes or heard his laugh. On her travels with her dad, she had been away for at least 4 weeks, and even whilst away, she had counted down the days until she could see him again. It was so unfair that she would never get that chance. There were so many things that she still wanted to say to him, so many ways she wanted him to know how much she cared for him, and how strong her love was for him. She never really had told him any of those things, because she never imagined that he would be taken away, so there was no need to tell him, all the time they were having fun and enjoying their lives.

Jessica decided she wanted to feel the wind against her face and breathe the fresh air into her lungs to revitalise her tired body. She made her way to the door and slowly walked down the steps, onto the sand. Being bare feet meant the sand felt chilled against her feet. Strong gusts of wind blew, causing Jessica to wrap her shirt around her tightly. She walked for several metres until she reached the shore line. There she stood for a while and looked all around her. The lights from the restaurants and cafes illuminated the sand in front of them, but otherwise the beach was engulfed in darkness, with no-one to be seen, except for the couple who became smaller and smaller as they walked away from Jessica into the distance.

Spotting a twig half hanging out of the sand, Jessica walked over to it and tugged on it forcefully, causing it to be pulled upwards. She brushed away all the tiny particles of sand that had become nestled in the small spindly pieces of wood at the end of the stick which had become frayed. Dropping to her knees, Jessica began drawing in the sand with her twig. Brushing in circles round and round, just like she had on the clay seahorse, she created patterns in the sand. Next she began forming a B. Soon she had spelled the word Blake, and put it in a circle. Stabbing the twig into the sand, next to Blake's name, Jessica sat back onto her bottom, and pulled her knees into her chest. Rolling onto her back, she spread out her arms and legs and looked up at the sky above. She could feel the cool breeze blowing across her belly which had been uncovered, as she gazed up at the shining stars dotted about in the sky above.

'Are you up there Blake?' Jessica asked in her thoughts, 'I wonder if you can see me now?' She thought. It was almost as though she willed for something to happen, like she wanted a reason to believe Blake could communicate with her. 'Come on Blake, do something' she thought. Waiting and watching, Jessica wanted to see a sign that Blake was there. Nothing happened. No star suddenly shone brighter, or rain beginning falling. No sound could be heard, except that of the waves, and no hand squeeze could be felt. All Jessica could detect with her sense was the normal sounds of the sea, and the coolness of the sand beneath her, and as she thought about it, she instantly began to shiver.

A little frustrated that nothing had happened, Jessica looked again at the word 'Blake' that she had written in the sand. Taking a sigh, she wondered where her parents had gone, as no one it seemed was in the house, because there was no light to be seen anywhere in the hut.

Jessica looked over at the hut. She could see lights on in the next beach hut along, Katrina's Jessica wondered if that was where her parents would be. She supposed so. Watching the yellow rectangular glow shining from the window in the distant beach hut, Jessica felt a surge of happiness. She had for some reason forgotten about the trip. Falling asleep in the afternoon and waking up in the dark had left her a little dazed and confused. Thinking about the school trip now made Jessica smile inside. She quickly got up, and brushed the sand off of her clothes, walking in towards her home. Stopping for a moment, Jessica looked out to the ocean one last time, and said out loud, "Night Blake. Love you."

Knowing she wouldn't hear anything back, she turned back and continued walking towards home.

Indoors, Jessica decided to leap straight into bed. Even if she didn't sleep, she just wanted to lie there and think about the trip to Sri Lanka and all that she would be able to see and do.

Chapter 15

The next morning, Jessica awoke earlier than usual. The clock on her bedside table displayed in its huge illuminated lights the figures 7.25 a.m. Feeling a dryness in her mouth, Jessica felt urged to get out of bed more or less straight after she had opened her eyes. Thrusting the summer duvet off of her body and stretching up to the ceiling, taking a large yawn, Jessica picked up her robe and walked out towards the living room.

There her mum was in the usual spot, stretching like a cat would, arching her back deeply, positioned on all fours. Beside her stood a mug of steaming green tea, sending wafts of its aroma into the air.
"Morning mum!" Jessica called, causing her mum to flinch and nearly lose her balance.

"Ah!" she squealed, "Morning Jessica!" her mum replied, in a funny voice caused by her stretching. It made Jessica smile a secret smile. She was so thirsty, she couldn't bear to wait much longer, and in a few moments was standing in the kitchen, drawing a class of cold water. She couldn't drink the water quick enough, taking huge mouthfuls until the glass was empty. Flicking the switch of the kettle and putting two pieces of sliced bread into the toaster, Jessica walked back into the living room to watch her mum, who this time was bending over to touch her toes.

"Did you have a good night last night mum? You weren't in when I woke up, and then I wanted to get to bed early. I think I'm still recovering from the time difference from travelling" Jessica asked.

"Yes, sorry darling. Meant to say, we went to see Katrina last night and ended up drinking several glasses of wine. You looked fast asleep when we left, we didn't want to wake you."

Jessica swallowed, feeling a little uncomfortable that she had perhaps been a little selfish, having been focused on her own feelings the last couple of days and not giving a second thought to Katrina.

"You know Katrina, she's a tough cookie. She's holding out - being ever so positive considering." Jessica's mum stopped stretching and looked up at Jessica who gave a few moments to think about the difficulties that Katrina faced. Her husband had also died when Blake was only a year old, and him being their only son meant the only company she would now have would be her own. Jessica tried to console herself a little by remembering Katrina had lots of friends. Their barbecues had always attracted many of the locals who Katrina got on well with. Jessica hoped she would be using them as company to console her grief.

"How are you sweetie?" her mum asked, looking curious. "You have been sleeping an awful lot!" she pointed out.

"As ok as I can be mum." Jessica returned with a hint of sarcasm. She didn't mean it, but it was a rather silly question to ask. How was she expected to be? And so what that she wanted to sleep a lot.

The sound of the toaster flicking up made Jessica's belly sound a grumble, and she hastily moved over to put it onto her plate. Her mother followed behind her. Spreading the butter onto the bread and watching it slowly melt and soak into the bread, made Jessica rush to get out the chocolate spread so that she could quickly finish dressing her bread and soon taste the sweetness on her tongue.

Realising a slight change in Jessica's mood and detecting that her questioning had perhaps caused it, Jessica's mum tried to change the subject, putting a tea bag into two mugs and filling them up with the steaming water, "How are you feeling about your trip away?"

"Yea, ok!" Jessica said, taking a bite of her toast. The chocolate tasted as amazing as she expected it would. Feeling ravenous, she devoured the first piece of toast in a matter of seconds, and quickly began spreading the butter onto the second piece.

"You know, we really are going to have to get a wriggle on with getting organised– there is so much to buy in preparation for you going away, especially if its next week!" her mother exclaimed.
Jessica nodded her head in agreement, seeing the teacher's organisational skills at work. She continued munching away on her crunchy toast.
"I thought about injections too. Luckily, because we went to Vietnam last year, I think you will be immunised for that area. But there are all sorts of other bits to get sorted." Her mum said. Jessica could tell her mum was apprehensive at the prospect of her going away.

Jessica continued to enjoy her toast whilst listening to her mum prattle on about everything she would need for her journey. Her mum handed her a mug of boiling tea, sending swirls of steam into the air. "We should write a list of everything…"
'Here we go!' Jessica thought to herself. It wasn't that she was not grateful, but sometimes her mother's anxiety got a little too much. She walked out of the kitchen and back into her bedroom, putting the steaming

mug onto her bedside table and flopping herself back onto her bed.

Pushing herself face down into the duvet, she cursed herself for being so ungrateful. Her mum had been so supportive over the last few days. She made a pact with herself that she would make a more concerted effort to be more positive in her responses.

Jessica felt tired again and wished she could go back to sleep now that her belly was full and felt comforted. She lay there for several moments, closing her eyes and pretending she was lying on the beach in Sri Lanka now with the sun blazing down on her body, warming her muscles.

She must have fallen into that dreamlike state when you are almost asleep, but not quite, because when Jessica opened her eyes again, it was 8.05am. Now she had to move sharpish, otherwise she would be late.

Within a matter of minutes, Jessica was showered, dressed and hastily walking out of the house and up the road towards school. The brisk walk went quickly and soon she was in the playground, met with the hustle and bustle of children everywhere, moving in all kinds of directions.

Deciding not to stop and chat, Jessica headed straight for Miss Button's office.
As she arrived at the blue door, she sternly gave three knocks. There was no reply. Three knocks again, and this time, she was greeted by Miss Button, sporting a smile that beamed from ear to ear.

"Good Morning. Sorry Jess I was just on the phone! And how are you today? Did you get chance to speak to your parents? What do they think? Are you coming?" Miss Button had obviously had too much sugar in her coffee Jessica thought, as the questions were coming thick and fast. She didn't know which one to answer first.

"Yes, Yes and Yes!" Jessica said, with an enthusiastic grin on her face. She watched Miss Button's reaction who immediately thrust her arms out to draw Jessica in for a hug.
"Brilliant! Wonderful! That is tremendous!" Miss Button exclaimed with dramatic conviction.

'Wow' Jessica thought. She was a little surprised at the over-zealous reaction. 'I wonder what's got into Miss Button!' Exuberance was an understatement. Jessica had never seen Miss Button so animated. She wondered if Miss Button was putting on a bit of an act to make her feel happy, because she felt sorry for Jessica. She was the sort of person who would do that – being such a lovely person, who cared deeply about her students. Jessica didn't at all mind even if it was a bit of an act. She welcomed the attention.

"Do you know Jessica, this is going to be the best adventure of your life so far. I guarantee it. "When you look deep into the eyes of those beautiful baby orang-utans who wrap their little tiny arms around you, gesturing for you to feed them, I can assure you will feel out of this earth." Miss Button said, again with flamboyance.

"I can't wait!" Jessica said. She had a burning desire to want to be there now and make those thoughts a reality.

"Well, I will ring your parents and inform them of what we need to do in preparation. In the meantime, you can go home!" Miss Button exclaimed.

Some Souls Live Forever

"Sorry?" Jessica asked, needing the statement repeated to check what she thought she heard really was true,

"You can go home Jessica!" Miss Button re-iterated. Mr Snithe and I thought, as it is only a week until you go away on this trip, we should see this as an extended break as that would be beneficial for you. We know it's been a little tough as it's been less than a week since you heard about Blake, so we thought maybe the best thing this school could do for you is let you be free for a little more time. That's if you want to of course!" Miss Button asked intrigued.

"Well, yes....I mean." Jessica began twiddling her thumbs and looking down and the green spotted carpet, "If I'm honest, I am finding it a little difficult being back, and I don't think I will concentrate much because I keep finding myself thinking about Blake." Jessica revealed.

"Listen! Come in!" Miss Button said, grabbing Jessica carefully by the arm and tugging her into the office. She closed the door behind her so that no one could hear. "Jessica, I'm going to tell you a secret, because I trust you that if I say you can't tell anyone, I believe that you won't." Miss Button looked at Jessica in a way that said she was going to say something important that needed Jessica's full attention.
"When I was your age, I lost my sister in a house fire. Grief is different for everyone, but I understand what it is like to lose someone special to you so suddenly. I know how that feels."

Jessica knew that Miss Button has been more understanding than anyone else, and Jessica felt she could talk to her more easily. Now it all made sense. It made sense too why Miss Button was such a lovely person, as she had been touched by a life-changing experience that had given her a different perspective on life about what truly mattered.

"Well Jessica," Miss Button continued, "I visited Mr Snithe and I told him that you would be finding it difficult to carry on as if everything was normal. So, I suggested it be better you have an extended break where you can go home and prepare for this trip. Then we can re-start school after you get back, when you will have lots to talk about and will feel full of beans again. What do you say?"

Jessica felt relieved. School had been hard. She felt like her personality had changed, and she didn't quite now how to fit back into her friendships, with her feeling in so much shock. It had only been a matter of days since she heard the news, and if yesterday was anything to go by, she wasn't going to be learning much because her thoughts were mostly needed for her to come to terms with the news and think about what had happened. The only lesson in which she had really engaged was English, and that was because she was writing about Blake.

"Thank you so much Miss Button. Thank you!" Jessica wanted to hug Miss Button again, but she felt a little embarrassed, feeling herself blush in the cheeks.

"Right then you, well, I'll be in touch with your parents. You just go home and look after yourself," Miss Button said, opening the door for her to leave. "Take care Jessica!" Miss Button called down the corridor after her.

Jessica was so glad that Miss Button had told her about her story. It meant Jessica knew that this trip away would be even more special, because now she could feel comfortable that someone would understand how she felt. She would understand how her mood fluctuated from one minute feeling extreme lows when she felt almost lifeless and desperately unhappy that Blake was no longer hear to hold her close, then switching to an overwhelming surge of energy that she knew she had to go out and live her dreams whilst there was still the chance.

Walking back out of school and back to home, Jessica felt more calm and relaxed. This is what she needed. Time and space to think and come to terms with what had happened, without having to think about stupid things that didn't matter anymore, like the number of degrees in a triangle, or the scientific explanation for the water cycle.

As Jessica realised she had a week at her disposal, she thought about what she would like to do for the next few days. She wanted to visit the caves where Blake and her had inscribed their names, she wanted to surf the waves and feel the buzz, she wanted to look through the photos of her and Blake and remember the happy times. All of this was what really mattered to Jessica, more than anything. She needed the time to let go and say goodbye.

Chapter 16

The next few days passed quickly. Jessica had spent most of the time preparing for her trip away, buying sun creams and mosquito sprays, walking boots and clothes for the rainforest. She had also visited all the places she wanted to go to, the special places that her and Blake had made their own since they were small toddlers. The tears had flowed, almost endlessly at times and the thoughts of sorrow had truly overcome her. Jessica had pondered over many things, she realised that at this moment, every time she closed her eyes and wanted to think of Blake, his face would came vividly to her, but Jessica was worried that in time she would forget what Blake looked like. She had devoted time compiling a photo album, with all her favourite memories captured on camera, which she decided she could look at any time she liked. She put this is a special green box stashed in the back of her wardrobe, which had several other mementos that were important to her.

Jessica was so glad that Miss Button had asked Mr Snithe for this time off for her away from the demands of school. Blocking out the emotions only to attempt to learn at school when she wasn't fully concentrating anyway, would only surely make matters worse and delay the grief. Of course she had every intention of returning to school, but only when she felt the time was right and she could cope with it.

Her parents had been more than happy at the agreement, as they were worried that the shock of the news and having to go back to school so soon would make it unbearable for Jess and only catch up with her in time, causing her to a belated and more difficult 'break down'.

Some Souls Live Forever

Soon, after the seven days and nights had passed, Jessica was ready to leave for Sri Lanka. It was on the way to the airport in a taxi with her parents and her teacher, that Jessica's excitement really began to build. As the car drew into the airport and the driver pulled their luggage out of the boot, Jessica stood to the side of the taxi and looked at her parents. She felt a little nervous that she was leaving them. Even though she knew Miss Button had a warm heart, she had never been away from her parents before.

"You enjoy yourself, and remember that we love you." Jessica's mum said, her voice quivering slightly, as she embraced her daughter tightly.
"Take some photos for your old man Jessie!" Her dad said, waiting his turn for his goodbye hug. Jessica threw her arms around his neck and hugged him tightly,

"Good luck dad, I'm so proud of you!" Jessica told him. Miss Button and her mum laughed.
"Shouldn't it be me telling you that?" he said, smirking. Jessica smiled. She looked at her mum who had watery eyes, but she was trying hard to hold it together.

"The World Conservation Trust will look after us, and soon Jessica will get to meet all the other pupils who are going on this trip too, so I'm sure she's going to love this!" Miss Button said, in an attempt to reassure Jessica's parents.

Both parents exchanged their "Thank you's" and made tracks to say goodbye. After one last hug from both of them, Jessica picked up her big blue rucksack, full to the brims and almost bursting at the zips. She slung it onto her back, which almost made her fall over with the weight! Walking into the airport with Miss Button felt a little strange, and especially looking over her shoulder to wave goodbye to her parents, but as soon as she took steps inside, they were met with a group of people who wore t-shirts displaying the World Conservation Trust logo.

"Hi! I am Miss Button, and this is Jessica, from Marylebone High School." Miss Button said to the volunteer, holding out a hand to be shaken.
"Hi guys, you have come at the right time, as lots of others have just arrived. Come on through to the lounge." The friendly looking volunteer suggested.
Jessica tentatively followed the tall brown haired man, wearing khaki shorts and an olive green t-shirt.

Meandering through crowds of people clutching baggage, they worked their way through to a glass encased lounge, where several other children Jessica's age were sat, accompanied by all sorts of adults. As Jessica walked into the lounge and the man showed her where to sit, she felt an edge of nervousness at having to meet new people.

Before she could give it much thought, she was shown to a seat which was adjacent to a small brown-haired girl wearing the same trainers as Jessica. Both the girls instantly noticed, looking at each others' trainers and then looking each other in the eye. Both of them smiled at each other at the co-incidence.

Miss Button was chatting to one of the reps, which meant Jessica was left alone. A small, brown haired, slender girl came over to Jessica and smiled again.
"Hi, I'm Nieve, What's your name?" the girl asked. She had a darker complexion, her dark hair hanging in ringlets around her neck. She had a friendly aura about her, that made Jessica feel she was a nice person.

"Jessica!' she replied "Are you going to the orphanage?" Jessica asked.
"I am, yes, isn't it going to be brilliant", Nieve said with excitement, revealing pure sparkling white teeth as she smiled.

Both of them sat next to each other, talking about their school and their favourite hobbies. Jessica found it was great to meet someone new who knew nothing about her sadness. It meant she could be someone else. She was like a blank piece of paper to Nieve, who knew nothing about her. This meant it was easier to talk, because Nieve had no reason to treat her any differently.

Miss Button soon joined Jessica and also began chatting to one of the other teachers venturing on the journey with one of his pupils.

The time ran away with itself, and soon it was time to board the plane. Jessica had forgotten completely that it was actually only 6.30am in the morning! Remembering this now meant checking through the security checks, and boarding the plane was done in a sleepy daze. Jessica couldn't wait to step onto the plane.

Chapter 17

Jessica slowly opened her eyes finding herself gazing out of the window of the plane, to be met with picture displaying a mixture of beautiful bright blues in the sky. Beneath the wing of the plane was a duvet of white fluffy clouds hung in the sky. As she peered further towards the window and gazed down at the sights below, Jessica saw the beginning of a sandy cove that encased a pool of turquoise shell coloured water. Stretched all along the glorious sandy beach were line upon line of exotic looking palms, which shimmered with their waxy surfaces shining in the glorious sun. The sun's orange glowing aura Jessica could see almost horizontally in line with the wing of the plane. She couldn't look at it for long, because its brightness was unbearable to watch.

Realising where she was, Jessica felt sensational. This was it – what life was all about. Making the most of moments like this. Jessica felt at peace with herself on her new journey into her future. It was her time now, to explore further all that life had to offer, and perhaps now with the understanding that life did not always deal the cards she expected them too, it was even more of a reason to enjoy life at every moment she could. She was living life for two people now, Blake and her.

Jessica knew deep in her heart that this did not signal a complete end to her sadness. She knew that at times it would feel almost unbearable that she missed Blake so much, but it was as though Blake was guiding her thoughts and making her believe in her future. She knew that is what he would want for sure. Looking again out to the tropical landscape below, Jessica felt completely at one with herself. Blake was her soul mate connected with her on a level that no one else had done, and right now she believed he was there.

Blake dying had been a tragedy for him, but his memory was set to live on forever. He was someone who had lived for the moment each and every day. His life was filled with laughter and a buzzing energy that everyone around him felt. Whenever Blake was in the room smiling, it made everyone smile, just like a ripple effect when a pebble is dropped into the ocean. He had a special soul that was set to influence the lives of everyone who knew him. Every time the people who knew him thought of him, they would remember the way he lived his life – like everything mattered, and that would remind them to do the same. This meant his soul could never die or be forgotten because it lived in the hearts of all those people.

Jessica thought about this for a few moments and realised that perhaps this is why he had been taken away so early. It would make an impact on everyone who knew him, and they would begin living their lives from now on more fully and completely, just had he had done. As Jessica contemplated this, she became comforted to know that there was a deeper meaning behind this sadness, and that positive light could be drawn from it if she searched hard enough. This gave her some hope for the future.

She realised then at that very moment that truly, some souls live forever.

www.ingramcontent.com/pod-product-compliance
Lightning Source LLC
Chambersburg PA
CBHW031216270326
41931CB00006B/581